Rachel of Old Louisiana

RACHEL

of Old Louisiana

AVERY O. CRAVEN

With illustrations by the author

LOUISIANA STATE UNIVERSITY PRESS • BATON ROUGE AND LONDON

Library of Congress Catalog Card Number 74–15921

Copyright © 1975 by Louisiana State University Press

Manufactured in the United States of America

Set in Linotype Garamond by G&S Typesetters,

Austin, Texas

Printed and bound by Kingsport Press, Incorporated,

Kingsport, Tennessee

Designed by Albert Crochet

ISBN 0-8071-2016-2 (paper)

The paper in this book meets the guidelines for permanence and
durability of the Committee on Production Guidelines for
Book Longevity of the Council on Library Resources. (∞)

Louisiana Paperback Edition, 1995
04 03 02 01 00 99 98 97 96 95   5 4 3 2 1

To Georgia
Who will understand

The plantation is in first rate order and nearly all planted. The corn is up and growing very pretty. The hands were sowing cotton all this week past. I hope a frost may not destroy it. My new orchard is my idol. I am afraid that I think too much of it all, and that God will punish me for letting my Heart cling to earthly treasures. I am not afraid to love the little black children. Christ suffered on the Cross for us all and it is my duty to take care of all that He has seen proper to place under my charge for His sake, which I do and love to do,—their mothers were all raised under my care.

—Rachel O'Connor

Contents

Preface		*xi*
1/	Old Louisiana	I
2/	Rachel, 1790–1828	I I
3/	Underway, 1824–1832	3 I
4/	A Woman Planter, 1830–1836	5 I
5/	In the Shadows, 1834–1840	7 I
6/	Evening, 1840–1846	9 I
	In Retrospect	109
	Appendices	I I 3

Preface

I met Rachel many years ago in an attic in Old Louisiana. I had been lecturing at Tulane University in New Orleans and could not resist the temptation to make my return to the North by way of Bayou Teche. While there, I had the good fortune to meet Weeks Hall and to visit his home, The Shadows, as he had restored it. I knew that he was an artist by profession, and I soon discovered that he was one of those rare souls who also made an art out of living. Yet as we walked about and talked of the Old South, my mind was always turning more and more to "higher things"— the attic. Weeks soon discovered the direction in which my feet kept turning and laughingly said, "Come back before you leave town and we will spend an hour together up there." I came back for my hour and stayed a week. It was an historian's paradise.

There I found Rachel. It was a case of love at first sight.

I copied some three hundred letters she had written to "Brother David" and promised Weeks that some day I would write a little book about her. The years have slipped by and now at evening time I come back to pay the debt contracted in the long ago. I have no thesis. It is still just a love affair.

My obligations are heavy. I must first give my thanks to Mrs. Stephen P. Dart, who also loves Rachel and who has searched out and copied for me the documents germane to Rachel in St. Francisville, Louisiana. Like a good historian she has selected the significant and ignored the trivial. Anne Plettinger, also of St. Francisville, has contributed both her knowledge and her rare skill with the camera toward bringing Rachel to life.

Farther back is the debt I owe Weeks Hall, who preserved Rachel's letters and those of her relatives and who had the good sense and patriotism to leave not only his papers but his home as well, for others to enjoy. (Rachel's letters are now housed in the Archives and Manuscripts Department at Louisiana State University, Baton Rouge.) I visited his home on many occasions and always ended up in the attic. I once wrote asking him to look in a certain trunk for a certain document that I wished to use. A week later that trunk came to my office at the University of Chicago by express with a note saying: "Look up your own document." That was Weeks all over.

There are no references included here because, after writing some ten books loaded down with footnotes, I just wanted to tell a story. The general information has been gleaned from forty years of research in Southern history. This is not a biography of Rachel. It is just a little book about her and the Louisiana in which she lived. The material available determined that slant.

A. O. C.
Dune Acres

1/ Old Louisiana

Rachel and her neighbors never called it by its name. They spoke of it only as "The River." That was their way of unconsciously saying that the Mississippi and its tributaries ran through their lives as well as through their lands. In fact, the lower part of Louisiana, in which Rachel lived, was a land that in geological formation was once a submarine deposit, then a prehistoric swamp, and finally an American kind of Netherlands.

Its deep, rich soils were made up of the sediment gathered from the whole interior of a vast continent and dropped as the rivers neared sea level, slowed down, spread out into bayous and shallow lakes, and reached the Gulf of Mexico through a tangle of marshes. Few places on earth have received so much alluvial soil, and few river valleys have matched those of Louisiana in fertility. Narrow strips of equal richness fringe her bayous and lakes, and a loess, just as fertile, is to be found on upland areas, such as West Feliciana Parish where Rachel planted her cotton and corn. Altogether they form one of earth's richest agricultural plots.

The Mississippi River and its lower reaches had been explored and settled by the French in their efforts to expand their American empire from Canada to the Gulf of Mexico. Disorder at home, however, had ended this dream and Louisiana, after a period under Spanish rule, came to the United States in 1803 by direct purchase.

In American hands the early efforts at the production of indigo and sugar were only moderately successful, and it was not until Étienne Boré, in the late 1790s, succeeded in making sugar from Louisiana cane that a new era dawned. The arrival shortly afterward of refugees from Santo Domingo, who brought with them a century-long experience in sugar making, gave the final impetus that created the matchless delta Sugar Bowl. With its rich river-valley plantations protected from flood by levees, with gangs of Negro slaves to dig and clear their ditches and to plant and harvest their crops, and with the steam engine to carry the load in the sugarhouse, the Louisiana sugar planter had indeed entered a new era.

Meanwhile, to the north and east of Baton Rouge, cotton farmers and speculators from the Old South were crowding in to form something of a frontier, which would in time be part of a Southern Cotton Kingdom. Elsewhere, back on the ridges, in the swamp forests, and on the pine hills and flats was another world which someone, by contrast, has called "the poor man's paradise." There owners and squatters found, in the timber, wood for fuel and for shelter and, on the open land, room for a patch of corn and pasture for their livestock. The gun would feed the family. Between these extremes were the people who lived in the towns or on the marginal lands. They might or might not have a few slaves. They did not envy the great planters, for they too had white skins.

Climate as well as soils played a part in making Old Louisiana a bundle of regions rather than a single social-economic unit. That part of the state lying south of thirty-one degrees latitude, where the Red River empties into the Mississippi, is a humid, subtropical region with an autumn rainfall of over fourteen inches. Sugarcane and citrus fruits of various kinds thrive there. The region north of this line has a temperate climate, a longer growing season, and a lighter rainfall in the autumn. It differs little from the climate of the Lower South and soon proved to be a natural home for cotton. The boll had time to open and the cotton-picking period was generally adequate. Best of all, these factors gave the small white farmers on the second river bottoms a chance to acquire a few slaves, to share in the profits when cotton prices were high, and to drop back into subsistence farming when cotton prices fell.

As a normal part of river-made regions, there was the old gateway city through which all things human and

material came and went. The marshes and the many out-
lets through which the Mississippi reaches the Gulf forced
the location of what became New Orleans, some seventy-
five miles upstream. From its very beginning it was unique
in people and in physical features. By the time Rachel
came to Louisiana, New Orleans was not just one city but
three cities in one. There was the original French town below Canal Street, little changed through the years in language, culture, or values. The streets were narrow and
lined with houses of French design. The Creole opera still
flourished and attracted European talent. Mardi Gras,
too, with all its color and abandon, was celebrated each
year, and the traveler who visited its markets and little
shops came away with the feeling that he had been in a
foreign country.

Just above the old town lay the bustling, growing
American city whose leaders dominated the business and
trade of the second-largest port of entry in the nation.
They dealt in sugar, cotton, and slaves and brought back
the furnishings just then so much in demand for plantation houses. They served as factors or merchants to whom
up-country produce was sent, perhaps to pay a debt due
for advances, or as agents on whom future drafts could be
drawn. They took care of the business side of planting and
thus served as the link between city and country groups.

Last, well out on the edges and sometimes in near
swamps, was a third city, neglected, tumbledown, and
slumlike, where the German and Italian immigrants

lived. They provided the labor which moved the cotton and sugar on which the prosperity of New Orleans depended. They toiled down on the wharves or uptown and, by their presence in the city, kept the population more white than black.

Put together these three cities revealed New Orleans as a bit of the Old World, a bit of the New World, and more of what the city itself had contributed. Nothing like it had ever before existed on American soil. It merited the adjective "fabulous."

"Fertile mud" and a favorable climate, or even a New Orleans, do not entirely explain antebellum Louisiana. The peculiar makeup of her population played an equally important part. Early settlement by the French, the importation of German laborers, and the arrival of some five thousand Acadian exiles laid the early foundations. Then came a heavy inflow of settlers from Mexico and the West Indies, especially from Santo Domingo, and, with a growing commerce, peoples from all parts of the Western world. New Orleans thus gradually became something of a racial-social melting pot. The Creole element, however, somehow still dominated and the Creole was always in the foreground. The Acadians, now called Cajuns, kept well to themselves, some prospering on their little farms, most sinking to peasantry. They grew in numbers if not in cultural influence.

The rural Creoles, on the other hand, by dividing their paternal acres among all male children, succeeded to a large extent in retaining both their blood and their culture. In the city they held aloof from Americans, and a few, in the rural world, kept their lands on the fertile river bottoms and were numbered among the great planters. Some writers have insisted that "civilization" in Louisiana, with its Mardi Gras and its opera, was always French at heart. That, perhaps, is true, but it is also true that in the end this civilization was lost in the swirl of American business and was soon spoken of as "decadent."

The most important change in Louisiana population, in the long run, was the result of the heavy importation of Negro slaves to toil in the cotton and the cane. The state was thus further divided not only into blacks and whites, but also into slaveholders and nonslaveholders. Assumed to be immune to malaria, the Negro found his place primarily on the fertile river-bottom plantations where he worked in gangs under an overseer. A more limited number toiled alongside their owners on the small, second river bottoms or served as domestics in the home.

Most of the great planters in Louisiana had once been farmers who had grown rich with the state itself or had been men of wealth when they came. Plantations, rich soils, and Negro slaves thus went together. They created what to the outside world was Louisiana. To begin with, the very fertility of the soil and its relative scarcity required an initial heavy investment of capital. The building of extensive embankments against flood waters and the constant digging and clearing of drainage ditches called for a labor force far beyond the demands of planting and harvesting crops. Furthermore, both sugar and cotton required expensive machinery to prepare their yields for market—gins for the cotton and grinding mills for the sugar. Only a rich man could buy and cultivate these river bottoms; only gangs of Negro slaves could supply the labor for what was a big business. By 1860 only a quarter of the free people in Louisiana lived in these so-called "black belts." Yet they owned half of the state's wealth, two-thirds of its Negro slaves, and nearly half of its large agricultural establishments.

It would be a mistake, however, to think of Rachel's world as being composed primarily of plantations, Negro slaves, and slaveholders. As a matter of fact, there were more farmers than planters in Louisiana, more white workmen than Negro slaves, and far more nonslaveholders than men who owned slaves. Even in New Orleans nine out of ten residents had no slaves; and in the black belts only about half of the families held slaves. The wealth of Louisiana thus belonged to a small upper class, and only about one in thirty-seven families belonged to this group. Most were planters, but bankers, factors, brokers, and lawyers living in the cities were closely allied with the planters and the business end of planting.

One final factor that played an important part in the life of Old Louisiana needs especial notice. Water was as much a part of her environment and resources as was her land. Her people traveled mostly by water. They sent their produce to market in boats. Their crops were a success or a failure according to the quantity or the time of rainfall. Most important, the lower reaches of great rivers prone to spring freshets, the shallow lakes, and the bayous and swamps scattered about everywhere were veritable breeding grounds for deadly germs and their insect carriers. All frontiers have had their health problems but Louisiana outranked them all. Malaria, ague, typhus, dysentery, cholera, and yellow fever took their regular tolls and created an atmosphere of perpetual alarm unmatched elsewhere. Reports of sickness and death filled family letters and local newspapers at all seasons. As late as 1850, Louisiana had the highest death rate of any state in the Union, and New Orleans of any American city. Death's door seemed always to be wide open and the number lying close to death alarmingly high. Health was always a major problem in Old Louisiana and among all classes.

Such was Old Louisiana in the days when Rachel Swayze came to this unique region, at a unique period in its life, to play a unique part in its development.

2/ Rachel, 1790-1828

There is an old saying that the frontier is a fine place for men but hell on women and oxen. Old as were some parts of Louisiana, her up-country, when cotton came tumbling in, revealed a raw, grasping, speculating quality matched on few American frontiers. It was here that Rachel O'Connor, lone widow, decided to go on planting in spite of the hell involved.

Rachel Swayze and her brother Stephen had come west to Louisiana in 1778 when their widowed mother, Rachel Hopkins Swayze, married William Weeks, already an established planter on Bayou Teche. Rachel was then only four years of age, and she certainly was not much over fifteen when she married young Richard Bell, bearing him a son and becoming a widow by eighteen. The next five years she spent at home with her mother, and it was at this time that she came to know and to appreciate her half brother David Weeks. In spite of a considerable difference in their ages, Rachel came to speak of him always as "My Dear Brother" and soon to rely on him in time of trouble. He seems to have taken her son Stephen Bell more or less under his care and, as time went on, the two boys began planning, someday, a sugar plantation on Grand Cote Island.

Stephen Swayze, Rachel's brother, was several years older than his sister and, when he received his share of the family estate, bought land in the Cotton Belt and began the life of a planter. We know little of him other than that he was twice married and that at his death in January, 1814, he left land and slaves and debts to be parceled out to a rather widely scattered group of heirs.

Rachel, meanwhile, had found new friends, and in 1797 she became the wife of Hercules O'Connor and went with him to begin life over again near Bayou Sara in West Feliciana Parish. As Rachel later wrote: "When we came to this place on the 13th of June, 1797, we had only provisions to last us two days and to trust in Providence for the next. Our meals had to be very scant and handled carefully, which learned us to be thankful for a little and value it much."

Since they began "very poor," a plantation in 1846 of more than a thousand acres and a goodly parcel of slaves must have been, as Rachel put it, "collected together by taking care of what is here." That was her way of saying that she and Hercules had worked hard and had kept their eyes open for more land and slaves whenever they came on the market. Travelers meanwhile told of "homes and gardens superb beyond description" in the region between New Orleans and Baton Rouge and spoke with contempt of the raw frontier to the north. There, they said, a new theory, not found in the works of political economy, was broached. Land, not metal currency, was the medium of exchange. Every crossroad and every avocation presented an opening, through which a fortune was seen by the adventurer in near perspective. "Credit was a thing of course. To refuse it—if this was ever done—were an insult for which the bowie-knife were . . . a means of redress." So prices rose like smoke and lands bought at the lowest government price were sold for thirty or forty dollars an acre and the state banks were issuing their bills in sheets. That was the atmosphere in which the O'Connors lived and created their plantation.

The cost, however, was heavy. The Louisiana environment had not changed, nor had the shallow waters lost their deadly germs and the mosquitoes that spread them abroad. Sickness and death were still a normal part of everyday life, and the frontier tangle of "boom and bust" kept the economic order in permanent confusion.

It should also be noted that, with hard work and limited amusements on this frontier as on others, heavy drinking had become common. Both Hercules and his son James had soon become addicts to the point of impaired health. The residents of Oakley plantation just across the way, where John James Audubon tutored the children, were therefore not surprised to be called suddenly one evening by the illness of Hercules. When they arrived they found him dead. Audubon remained all night with the corpse, and it is from him that we learn that "the poor man had literally drank himself to death." The son James was evidently no better, for in May, 1822, Rachel had him interdicted, saying that he was "afflicted with habitual infermaty," which totally unfitted him for any kind of business and "renders him incapable of taking care of his property." That was a nice way to saying he was a confused alcoholic. He too was soon dead.

Thus in the years between 1814 and 1822, death took Rachel's brother Stephen Swayze, her husband Hercules O'Connor, and her sons Stephen Bell and James O'Connor. Each death brought new problems and laid burdens on Rachel's shoulders that would have tested the courage of the toughest frontiersman.

She was in a desperate situation. She was now alone with a plantation and its slaves on her hands. Should she do as she had done once before—go home to her mother—or should she go ahead and accept the unique place of a woman planter in what was clearly a man's world? She did not hesitate. She would stay right there. She would shoulder the problems.

Stephen Swayze left two young daughters "at present in a very helpless situation without parents or a brother old enough to take charge of their property." There was only one way out. Clarissa and Charlotte became part of Rachel's household, to be cared for, sent to school, and given all the advantages of a Southern home. They always spoke of Rachel as "My Mother." She, in turn, always referred to them as "My Girls."

Her son Stephen left an even greater burden. He had gone with David Weeks to develop their sugar plantation on Grand Cote Island but had soon wearied of the undertaking—it was too lonesome there. After a short trial he sold his share in the project to David and departed posthaste for the more exciting New Orleans. There he undertook what he called "merchandizing" and, while David went on to make a fortune in sugar, Stephen failed miserably and piled up enormous debts, which threatened Rachel with financial ruin to the end of her days.

Unfortunately, one of those whose claims on Stephen ran into thousands of dollars was William Flower, whose brother Henry had married Pamela Weeks, Rachel's half sister. That complicated matters that were already bad enough. In November, 1820, just before Stephen's death, William Flower instituted a suit against Rachel as "Representative of your son's estate." He knew, of course, that the estate consisted primarily of debts. He also knew that Rachel, as Stephen's mother, was the only property holder involved. So when Rachel responded, he withdrew his suit and proposed that either he be permitted to "look into the management of Stephen's estate" to see that it "should be put into the hands of some discreet person" who would pay off the creditors "in proportion to the amount of their claims" or, as an alternative, that "such money as come-in from the estate" should be held as "collateral security for the amount due the creditors." He later claimed that Rachel had accepted the alternative proposal and had said that she would pay all of Stephen's debts. He then suggested that she begin payments at once. She foolishly complied by turning over to him some notes due Stephen. The next year, when another "note of Bell and Finley for $5,000" came due, he again "urged payment." It was a tragic year for Rachel, but she was somehow able to send him $3,100, which, as he said, "he placed to her credit."

Then came the staggering blow. In 1822 Flower announced his retirement from business and that all debts due him must be paid immediately with accumulated interest at 10 percent. He said he hoped that if Rachel's notes, now in his hands, were "good and solvent," *her* debts might be diminished to eight or ten thousand dollars. It was thus quite clear that, with Stephen's death in 1821, he thought he could pressure Rachel into meeting any or all of his demands regardless of their legal soundness or her ruin. Rachel, in alarm, had already turned to David. Realizing her helpless position, David suggested that she "sell" her plantation to him with the understanding that she should remain there and manage all its affairs as long as she lived. In this way, Flower would be forced to deal with a man and his lawyers, not with a lone woman.

Flower at first seems to have accepted this situation and to believe that David would assume Rachel's "responsibilities." Only gradually did he learn that he now faced lawyers who knew their business and would accept only what was legal. Yet, as late as October, 1824, Rachel wrote David that she "had the honor of meeting Wm. Flower at a relative's home and that he was very friendly." He pulled his whiskers, laughed, and said that he had heard she was "agoing to outcrop them all." Her only comment was, "How glad I should be if I could get clear of that man." Unfortunately she could not. He now firmly believed that Rachel's sale of her plantation to David was simply a subterfuge and that title to the property still remained in her hands. He would ignore David. For the time being things remained this way, but trouble threatened. Rachel seems to have retained some property in her own name and not to have included all her slaves in the "sale." She had, moreover, recently cleared title to land "that formerly belonged to [her] poor James." She thus felt secure and able to go on managing the plantation that she and Hercules had created. There was, in fact, no other place to go.

Cotton planting in Louisiana was, as we have said, big business. It involved machines and a variety of supplies. The head of such a business had to know the soils and the best methods of planting, tending, harvesting, and marketing crops. Overseers might share a part of the responsibility but the "master" was responsible even for the overseer and the labor that he directed. More important than the material side was the creation and continuation of an atmosphere of cooperation and harmony. It was, as the saying goes, a man's job. Few women would have undertaken it. But Rachel O'Connor was no ordinary woman. She had gone through difficult years and great tribulations, which had not broken her spirit. She knew men both black and white and troubles small and large, and she still believed that there was a God somewhere in the universe who shaped all things for the best. Health seemed to be the only problem that had not been solved.

In August, 1823, Rachel wrote of being very sick for five or six days "with the ague and fever." Her eyes were so weak that "it was troublesome to write." She was growing weaker every day, she said, which made her afraid to put off writing when a short time might "put her out of power to do so." Death had already taken five of her neighbors and "two others were lying at the point of death." She was, she said, unable to finish the letter because her chills and fever were so bad that she could not "set up." She closed by saying: "Should we never be permitted to see each other on this Earth, my blessing will remain with you, farewell. Let me know how the negro shoes are to be got. I expect they will commence picking cotton tomorrow morning."

That autumn a yellow-fever epidemic spread northward out of New Orleans and "carried off a great many for so small a place as Saint Francis Ville." Rachel was certain that the "Steam Boats" were responsible for its spread in her neighborhood and was very thankful that they could not, at this time of the year, get near her relatives. She was highly indignant when she learned that, on the death of a young neighbor boy, Dr. Barton "took the liberty of opening him, both *body and head*, removed his *stomach* and carried it home with him." She thought the doctor should be sued and "given all the trouble possible." It never entered her mind that medical research might be involved.

Rachel herself had been "very unwell" all year, but those who plant cotton cannot take much time off for being sick. Cotton, like time and the tides, awaits no man. So, as soon as the bolls began to open, Rachel's slaves were in the field with the cotton bags, which she had made that winter, over their shoulders. As they moved down the rows, her early prospects for a good yield grew dim. The "late rains" had rotted much of the cotton and the return would be no better than that of other years. She was "done with boasting of her great crop."

Then, to make matters worse, the gin, which she had just "put in shape," went bad and valuable time was lost while she searched for a mechanic and repairs could be made. In the end Rachel had only 75,000 weight on her books "with only a very little more to pick." So she put a part of her force to clearing land, and as soon as the axes were ready she sent the rest of her men. The women and children could finish the cotton. Meantime, she had hired an overseer at $25 per month. She would try him out for two months and if he behaved well she might hire him for the coming year at $150.

So the years moved along—planting and harvesting, with fickle nature always promising a little more than was delivered. By the first of December, 1825, she had "all the crop gathered except some scattering cotton that old Milly and Leah and the children" would finish in a few days. In all she had forty-seven bales prepared and some "yet to gin." She could at least "have a faint hope of having corn enough to last out the year." In the meantime she had started the hands "to burn and chop in the log ground." She hoped to get more "chopped down" after the logs were rolled. She would then have new land for planting.

She had done well but it was quite evident that some neighbors resented a woman planter, for in early December of that year she wrote David: "Do pray come over here next month. If you can stay only one week, it will convince the people that you are not tired out with my troubles, which I am sure there are many praying for."

In late January, 1826, Rachel wrote that she had not been away from home "on account" of one of "my negro women being near having a young one, which was born on the 19th instant and is this evening Dieing. I sincerely lament its poor mother's distress. P.S. . . . My little negro babe is Dead."

There was, however, little time for grief. The fields

were calling. The price of cotton was down and Rachel found it necessary in the months ahead to give more and more attention to the slaves at work in the fields. It was on such an occasion that she had an experience that is best described in her own words: "At one oclock, I returned home from the fields, after taking a long ride all through them, in as good health as I ever was, only very warm; set in the gallery (at least a quarter of an hour) to have some water drawn out of the well, and then took a drink, and in a few minutes fell senseless on the floor." She was not seriously injured, she said. One foot pained some, her temples were bruised, her breast was a bit sore and painful when she took a deep breath.

Her real trouble was a growing fear of being "taken off" suddenly by another such attack. With that in mind she wrote a letter to her brother David, in which she gave detailed instructions for the disposal of her property in case of sudden death. When her "Just Debts were paid," she wrote, her property should be divided into four equal parts—one-fourth to David, one-fourth to the heirs of Stephen Swayze, one-fourth to her half sister Pamela, and the last fourth to be divided equally between "My Dear Mary Clarissa Swayze" and "my poor Brother Caleb's" son William James. (Caleb Weeks was another half brother; see Appendix I.)

The interesting things about her plans were that Clarissa's share was to be a Negro girl by the name Caroline, a daughter of Patience and Y. [B?] Sam, and that the plantation was to be sold with the stock of horses and cattle and everything else *"except the poor negroes."* She insisted that they "be kept amongst the heirs of my Dear Mother." She went on: "Patience has been a faithful Slave to *me*, and mine, in all my distresses for twenty-two years, for which I should be glad you would let her stay with any part of her family that she chooses . . . and not considered a slave any longer than I live. . . . And Pless has been a great relief in my late trouble both in sickness and health, for which I should be glad for her to be indulged in like manner . . . which is all I have to say on the present Melancholy Subject."

As an afterthought she asked that, if her horse were still alive at the time of her death, David take him home and keep him there as long as he lived. The horse was not to be considered part of her "property." Fortunately, Rachel suffered no more fainting spells and life on the plantation went on as usual.

As the 1820s were coming to an end, a depression, national in sweep, began to be felt in trade and agriculture alike. "Hard times" did not reach a peak until the mid-thirties but cotton already had begun to feel the pinch. That perhaps accounts for the fact that William Flower and his brother now increased their pressure for a settlement with Rachel. Her lawyer Mr. Turner assured her in early December, 1827, "that he still thought he could settle the debt for her very easy." It was only necessary for her "to petition the Probate Court to allow an inventory of the property necessary to be taken." This would clear her "of being accountable for the debts." Rachel immediately took this step and "Mr. Turner and Mr. Swift," on December 8, began "to take an inventory of Poor Stephen's Books, or at least of his estate, from his books."

At this point, for a time, Rachel seems to have wavered. Her lawyer, however, insisted that "it would not do for her to attempt to move" until she was entirely "clear of debt." To do so she would have all her troubles to go over again. If she would stay on a few years longer, all her debts would be settled. So Rachel visited her family "on the Tech" and came home to find her overseer "laid up with the Plurisy" and Old Daniel to have saved "a little over 25 dollars" for her. He had, she added, tended the garden very well. The overseer informed her that he expected 120 bales of cotton, but Rachel, with a feeling that her whole world was tumbling down, did not expect so much.

Then on May 29, 1828, the storm that had been brewing broke over Rachel's head. In a personal letter of more than four thousand words, William Flower expressed "the indignation" that he felt toward her at "the tricks, shifts, evasions and quibbles of the Law" which had been practiced on him for the past six years "in relation to the debt due us by the estate of S. Bell." *He* was certain that she was not ignorant of "the deceit, intimidation, and defamation being practiced in order to defraud him of his just rights; but since some of her relatives insisted that she was innocent, he now, against the advice of his counsel, was "determined to state . . . the reasons for believing that the conduct towards us has been ungenerous and unfair." Then followed a long, detailed account of her promise and agreement and of how her lawyers had entered pleas aimed only at delay. They had even argued that Rachel, as a married woman, had made her commitments without the consent of her husband, so they were in no way now binding. Thus, while he, William Flower, had been fair and generous, her lawyers had adopted methods used only to delay a settlement and to cheat him out of his "just rights."

Rachel's reaction to this abuse came in a letter to "Brother David":

> I did a few days since, receive a long epistle from Mr. F. wherein he expressed the indignation he felt towards myself and friends. . . . I expect you have some liesure hours to spare and would like something new to read to pass off the time pleasantly, from which I have concluded to enclose for your perusal, a true copy of his letter to me. The original I have sent to Mr. Turner to answer if he thinks proper to do so. . . . I feel too small to undertake a letter to a person so high standing in life as Mr. F., although I suppose he wishes me to do so, and commit myself too. But he scarcely will ever catch me naping again, so long as I can keep my senses.

So, with threats of suits still hanging over her head, Rachel went forward with her plans for the coming year. She was confident that, if outsiders would keep their hands off, all would be well. Her plantation, in spite of bad weather, was in fine shape. The late frost had made her corn look extremely bad but she was certain that, if cotton-seed could be planted early enough, this could be a banner year. She had made 111 bales of cotton last year and all was now sold. Only the Flowers and their efforts disturbed her. They had appealed, and the suit was to be tried again in New Orleans. She only hoped she would fare as well this time as she did the last. She had discovered however that, even after having vented his "indignation" in an angry letter, William Flower was more angry with her than usual. He was now threatening to publish "the whole affair" between them, "which he says will disgrace me in the eyes of the world." He had said that unless she were "very, very cautious blood would be spilt." Her lawyer Mr. Turner, however, seemed "quite at ease, and firm as ever" on Rachel's side.

This was comforting, but just now she could not bother with lawsuits. Her corn crop, in spite of the frost, looked promising, but to offset this she was having trouble with her overseer. They had "quarrelled twice of late. He thinks himself a much bigger man since his marriage," she said, "and I will be glad when his time is out, to get clear of him."

During the next three months, Rachel did not inspect her fields. This was due, she said, to the fact that her "horse had a sore back" and "to an unfriendly feeling towards my overseer." They had not agreed well for several months, and she knew him to be too obstinate to do any better with her looking after him, so she concluded to let him have his own way, only mind that he did not abuse the Negroes and horses. That had been the only reason for their quarrels. But "today," she added, "I have freely forgiven *all* within my own breast,—my cotton crop appears so uncommonly promising. Indeed I do think that I may expect 150 bales, if no accident should prevent." She would have a large yield while other planters in her neighborhood were saying that they could not expect one-half of a crop!

For a time Rachel had been worried because "her girls" did not show "the least appearance" of "changing their situation in life." She would rejoice greatly if the eldest of the two were married but neither showed much interest. Her worries, however, were needless, for Charlotte was soon married to a Mr. Doherty and on "the evening previous to New Years," 1830, her dear little Clarissa and Lewis Davis, "the best of young men," clear of debt, owning nine Negroes and three thousand in cash, were wed. They would live in the old Swayze home. Just now, however, the two girls were busy dividing their father's estate with their brother William. Each sought Rachel's advice, and she was especially anxious for Brother David to take over Clarissa's share, because she was only "a poor little orphan girl and it is our duty to take care of her, at least, for a while." Both girls would have chosen to let things remain as they were, until debts on the estate were paid, but their brother William dashed about "dressed fine, feared no expenses, agreed to follow every friend's advice, and then went his own way at last." He was soon in love and married, but with no idea of how to make a living.

So Rachel's life had gradually fallen into a pattern required to manage a plantation in this turbulent young-old Louisiana. Most of her time and thought were taken up with looking after the planting, the tending and marketing of her cotton, the buying of supplies, and the directing of her forces. She had hired and released overseers, looked after her slaves in sickness and health, and watched their increase and sometimes loss in death. She had also been forced to look after the legal problems that her son Stephen's debts had thrust upon her. There was scarcely a term of the district court in the 1820s and early 1830s in which Rachel did not face a suit for some debt—a situation complicated by the fact that her agent for collection of funds and payment of debts sometimes used her money for his own purposes. His sudden and unexpected death therefore left Rachel forced to pay debts for which she had already provided funds. The opinion of the court was that, "granted her agent had abused her confidence and had defrauded her, she had trusted him and must bear the consequences of her indescretion. The rule is, who trusts must lose."

In spite of all of Rachel's troubles, her love for her plantation and her Negroes outweighed them all. She had seen the land turn from prairie to plantation, and she had seen her Negro babies grow from the cradle to the status of full field hands. "If you could see the Old House yard just now," she said, "you would understand." The crape myrtle trees were in full bloom, perfectly red and surrounded by other flowers and shrubs. "I don't think it ever before looked so pretty. I do pray that there may not come a storm of wind to blow down all the beauty that I so dearly love, as it happened once before when I admired greatly. Indeed I must acknowledge that I blame my own vanity for the storm being sent to destroy my pride and vain glory. Now, I hope, I have better feelings for I know that I deserve no part of the praise. It all belongs to my God the bestower of all good." But the land without the Negroes would, for Rachel, be an empty paradise. God had placed these poor creatures under her care, and she loved them as a mother loves her children, nursed them·in sickness, saw them dressed comfortably, and never asked for more of work than they could reasonably provide. Night after night the sick ones slept in her own room under her personal care. Day after day those who were unfit were kept out of the fields. Even when Brother David asked that she divide her labor force and send a portion to him, she drew back. He could take them all, but the old Negro women would grieve so much to part with their boys that she really could not undertake to send the few. Even as it was, the old ones made such long, sorrowful faces that she had made up her mind it was all or none.

3/ Underway, 1824-1832

The institution of Negro slavery, always a tangle of contradictions, spread over Rachel's Louisiana like a dark shadow. Negroes were both *property* and *human beings*. The property side was taken for granted; the human side was largely an afterthought.

Kind-hearted Rachel, caught in this tangle, once wrote of her sister's "fine luck" in having "five little negroes born in less than two months' time, and two more women that expected to be confined hourly." Her reaction was clearly that of a planter viewing the increase of Negro babies as she might have viewed an unusual litter in the barnyard. Yet it was the same Rachel who wrote of her "sixteen little negroes arising" and her little Isaac, who "is subject to a cough but seldom sick enough to lay up. . . . The poor little fellow is laying at my feet, sound asleep—I wish I did not love him as I do, but it is so, and I cannot help it."

At an earlier time when she feared a sudden stroke, Rachel had recognized the human sides of Patience and Pless and wished them not to remain as property after her death. Yet, in the very same document, she had given a Negro girl to her niece Clarissa, just as she might have given a piece of furniture or a dress. She was clearly not yet ready to face the tangle. Nor were her neighbors. Almost every incident involving the two races revealed that fact. Yet Rachel in her own way saw the difficulty when she wrote her brother David that "nothing had yet been done to the molatto man" who was believed to have murdered a Negro woman on the road. "Perhaps," she added, "they may hush it up to save their negro from being hung." She was clearly saying that property stood in the way of social justice and implying her disapproval.

Rachel again saw the contradiction involved when "the negroes over at Thomson [Thompson's] Creek" had some idea of rising "and had the business planed" when a Negro woman informed on them and had "a stop put to their wickedness by hanging two negroes." She wrote, "A search had been made for one or two white men" involved "but they had escaped so far." The report was that "there were two more negroes that had ought to be hung" if justice had taken place, but their masters were rich, "which proved excuse enough to save them."

The Negro himself seems to have been unusually conscious of his human rights in this period when the corn supply was short and the whites were themselves restless.

The situation was indeed a serious one for both races. Rachel was so worried that she scarcely knew whether she "was living or not" and sometimes feared that she and her people "must all starve, when her potatoes were all eaten." Most of her time, she said, had to be spent in the search for corn.

Others must have been in the same situation, for as Old Daniel and B. Sam were coming through Jackson with some of Rachel's corn, a white man was seen buying from them. For this the people of Jackson seized him and made him ride a pine pole through the streets and "when his wife made a fuss about it, they put her on the same pole and gave them a ride together." For Daniel's part, Rachel had him demoted to field-Negro status, which "sunk his spirits very low." Much as she valued her gardener, she knew that this was no time to loosen the reins of slavery.

Reports of Negro crime and disorder came closer and closer, and one night a band of runaways entered and robbed the home of one of Rachel's nearest neighbors. Two of the robbers were caught and some of the property recovered, but more runaways from the same group, when shot at by a man who lived "in the Plain, watched until they caught one of his young negro men, cut off his legs and arms . . . pulled out his eyes, and left him to bleed to death." It was then discovered that there were twenty-five or more runaways in a nearby swamp, "all armed men." A posse of whites went in search, finding and killing eight or ten of them just as they would have hunted and killed wild animals. On David's own island ten slaves attempted to run away, but a peddler turned them back amid rumors of slave uprising floating about on all sides. One report of a Negro rebellion on Robert Barrow's plantation send an army of men to the rescue. When they arrived, to their disappointment, they found the overseer and his men peacefully at work in the fields. Rachel proudly wrote her brother that when her overseer Patrick was asked to go on this expedition he refused, saying that his place was here at home when trouble threatened.

It was a wise decision, for there was already trouble at home. Mrs. Bowman, another of Rachel's neighbors, lay at what "might have been her Death Bed." On the previous Sunday night she had found fault with one of her female servants and had undertaken the task of chastising her. The girl, however, had returned blow for blow and had proven too strong for her mistress. The slave had thrown her down and beaten her unmercifully on the head and face, "which swelled greatly and turned so black that one could not have recognized her."

The girl, meanwhile, had been seized and Rachel was certain she would be hanged. She was an uncommonly smart yellow woman and a first-rate house servant. Mrs. Pirrie had bought her in New Orleans and had used her as a waiter and nurse until her own death. The girl had then become the property of Mrs. Bowman, who until now had found her excellent in all ways. Rachel was certain that some mean white man was back of all the trouble. "What a pity," she said, "that he was not black." It is interesting to note that when "hanging time" came, Mrs. Bowman pleaded so hard for the girl's life to be spared that the officials yielded, or pretended to do so, and said that the girl would be "shipped" to New Orleans and confined for life in a dungeon or "put to ball and chain."

Meanwhile, throughout the summer, reports of racial troubles continued. The newspapers were filled with stories of Negro unrest and of outsiders openly stirring up rebellion. A Negro preacher on Mr. Swift's plantation had burned all the Negro houses and had then run away with most of his slaves. This had come so close to home that the men of Rachel's parish were raising money by subscription to hire an armed guard to ride the roads day and night. Such a condition, along with a wave of yellow fever, kept tension high. Rachel confessed that her feelings were so overcome between hope and fear that she was afraid to open a letter from her own relatives. She would put it in her bosom and walk about for several minutes before she ventured to do so. Even then, she skipped hastily to the last page, to make certain there was no bad news, and then turned back to read it all.

Yet, in spite of everything, Rachel insisted that she was not alarmed. As she put it, she had not raised her Negroes "that way or to such principles." She then added that Bridget had had a fine boy on the sixth and that Mrs.

Gaitree had run off with a clerk from her husband's store, leaving four little children worse off than being motherless.

What should be remembered is that this part of Louisiana was going through its unique frontier experience of land and labor exploitation. Hard drinking and physical violence went with this experience on most frontiers. Rachel was only reporting the normal when she wrote that Tom Chaney "slipped up" on old Mr. Coursey's son when he was eating supper and "struck him dead. He then took all his own negroes and ran off." She had heard of no reason for the act other than that Tom was drunk. A short time later she reported that Dr. Hern's lady was stabbed in the back while sitting at her window and that a man walking along the riverbank was shot in the head by someone on a passing boat.

Then, as a kind of climax, Rachel told of how Mrs. Higgenbotham had been put in jail in Clinton along with the man who had shot her husband. The authorities had gotten her there only by telling her that she must go to Clinton to lay claim to the property belonging to her late husband. In the next mention of the case, Rachel noted that Mrs. Higgenbotham had stood trial and had "come off clear, by some means, not well understood by her neighbors, who were greatly displeased at her good luck." Some were saying that the acquittal was due to the judge being a Frenchman, not properly acquainted with the English language so as to understand the charge against her. Not a woman in Clinton would let her enter their doors and she was ordered from several homes where she had expected to be received kindly. The man who was accused of killing Mr. Higgenbotham was also "set at liberty" to the astonishment of the whole community.

The constant harassment to which Rachel was subjected by the Flower brothers and the quick seizure of "Poor Caleb's" property before his widow could enter her claims were, in turn, only other expressions of this unique agricultural frontier. They were part of the hell that women and oxen might expect.

Yet Rachel was not discouraged. Her health had become so good that she had almost forgotten her age, and she could boast of her ability to attend to her affairs with ease. She was even urging her brother to purchase another tract of land nearby. Her overseer Patrick had done the best he could and had behaved so well that she was glad to engage him on the same terms for another year. The plantation was now in good shape, "the whole under good fence and every part of the work managed with ease." Her cotton had sold well and Patrick was now clearing new land. She therefore had "no kind of uneasiness about either fields or negroes." So, as she put it, "I am still trying to creep along slowly with the help of good friends bestowed by a kind God. My trust is in my God, who orders all right. It is my duty that his will should be my pleasure, and I sincerely *Pray* that fortitude may be granted me to obey."

But such a period of peace and progress could not last long in Rachel's troubled world. Soon she was praying for her "Good Brother" to "make every haste to get here" that was in his power. Pamela's husband Henry Flower was behaving "so meanly" toward her and her brother Stephen's orphaned children that she had begun looking on him as being as great an enemy as his brother. He had already brought a suit against her for her son Stephen's debts and she could "not bear the idea of H. F. and his friends enjoying the pleasure of breaking" her "up which was their mutual wish."

"Do my dear Brother," she wrote, "come and help save all you can. It is thought that a short time will make it forever too late for us to do anything towards securing the property out of the power of D. [H.?] and Wm. F." Her "adversaries" had lost all feeling for others. They did not care how much cost she was "run to." So she watched the road constantly for her brother's coming although she knew that it was too soon to expect him. She was, she said, so troubled that she was ill and her only comfort came from the fact that her dear Clarissa had married a good man— Clarissa, the only being on earth who was left to call her "Mother."

Brother David did come and some temporary adjustment was reached. For the present, at least, Rachel could find comfort in the fact that work on the plantation was going smoothly. The cotton and the corn were nearly planted and, in spite of a sore throat, Patrick continued attentive to his business. The Negroes were all well and the teams in fine shape. She could not, however, leave home because of her Negro children—"two of them sucking babes and two more soon expected." And besides, her "poor little Isaac" had been seriously ill, and she had kept him and his mother in her own bedroom each night. Busy with her garden and with fifty or sixty little chickens hatched and thirteen hens setting, she had little time to go visiting, much as she might wish. She did, however, take the time to tell her brother that the roads were so deep in mud that several "pine woods oxen" had mired down and had been left there to die. Rachel's sympathies naturally were with the oxen.

Patrick meanwhile had begun his last year and was as industrious as usual. He had 129 bales of cotton pressed and expected some 30 or 40 more. He had cleared over 30 acres of land that winter and could always be counted on to raise a good crop when possible. Even her neighbors followed his planting methods. He was, indeed, the best of farmers, careful of the "work-horses," but inclined "to treat some negroes better than others"—a remark that led her to note that black Susie's eldest daughter had recently had a baby, which "made three mulattoes born this year and still alive." It was not, however, until Patrick was gone at the end of the year, due in part to financial reasons, that Rachel spoke out: "Patrick behaves too mean to be a white man. His tracks are often found where he has been sneaking out after those negro girls." She had evidently known this all along, but his skill as a farmer had muted this side of Negro slavery.

For the present, though, she let Patrick go his own way even when she did not always approve of what he was doing. She was too occupied with the "unfortunate affairs" with the Flower brothers to bother with Patrick. Referees had been appointed for a settlement, and Mr. Turner had been busy gathering the documents needed for her defense. She somehow felt that an agreement was near, and she was confident that if this "troublesome settlement proved any way easy" she could then attend to all her other duties with ease. She was so distressed about it that she could "scarcely describe her feelings,—which made her hate herself" for having once been "so simple." Her heart trembled at the very thought of court opening the first of May.

And well her heart might tremble. Things did not go well for her in that session, and a sheriff had already visited her, authorized, he said, to seize property to satisfy claims against her. His first order was to demand money, at which she told him that he might do so but it was well known that necessity had obliged her to sell all and every part of property she owned on earth to pay her just debts. She had paid her money as far as it would go to those she justly owed. "He appeared," she said, "to study very seriously for some time, and then went away."

Meanwhile, her agent had found where her sale to "Brother David" was recorded "in the mortgage book where all mortgages remained until paid." Next morning early, she went with her agent to the clerk's office and released the mortgage, acknowledged the notes paid, and was home before the sheriff returned "to perform his duty by levying an execution on all he could find" that belonged to her. She then informed Mr. Turner of the manner in which the sheriff had acted and requested his advice. He wrote her at once, saying that the sheriff had no right to levy writs on the property and would "lay himself liable to an action of Damages by her brother David, if he did so." Turner further told her that the sheriff in her absence could not open her doors if locked and that he could not take anything from the plantation even should he levy on it. For the present, at least, she need not worry. Turner would at the right time apply for an appeal for putting off a trial.

So Rachel could turn her attention to the plantation, where Mr. Mulkey, her new overseer, "was behaving very well" and managing his business with ease. He was "really a smart man on a plantation." She could at least be certain that no white person troubled the Negro quarters now and that the distemper that was killing her neighbor's cattle had not spread to her plantation. Her one worry came from the wave of cholera sweeping the region. She had bought three barrels of lime with which to whitewash all the Negro houses. She was having "their bedding and the houses aired often, their clothing kept clean, their vic-

tuals" cooked done "and their milk churned every morning to have it sweet for them." She was even thinking of
giving her own "old house a brushing over" with lime, to
see whether it would do any good.

She was quite well at the present but "much frightened
at the dreadful news of the *Cholera* being so near as New
York and Philadelphia or even nearer." Neighbors were already preparing for it by storing medicine considered useful against this dreadful disease. She had written to a Mr.
Linton for whatever might be best, for as long as she
lived, she would not let the Negroes suffer for anything
she could do for them. Some people were buying "flannel
to make negro shirts" to wear next to their skin. If that
proved beneficial she was willing to try it.

The cholera scare, however, had not kept the "Flower
Brothers" from their efforts to secure by force what they
claimed was their "just dues." Late in September Rachel
had written her brother David about "the unfortunate
situation" of his affairs over here. The sheriff had "levied
an execution" on the cotton she had sent to the river landing and intended to come out to the plantation to "do the
same" with the rest. In desperation she now sent Arthur
off with a letter begging David to come at once and then
hurried over to the home of her lawyer, Mr. Turner. She
found him also greatly disturbed and not certain that he
had been given sufficient authority to act. Yet he assured
her that he "had hopes of making them repent their rash-

ness." He agreed with Rachel in urging David to start at once, for there was no time to lose. Frightened "out of her wits," she hurried home to prepare as best she could for the hell that would come on "the morrow."

What happened the next day is best described in Rachel's own words as written to David:

> In all my difficulties I never had so great a fright. My heart almost failed [when] the Sheriff came and seized all the cotton on the plantation and part of the negroes. . . . Twenty-five bales were hauled to the landing, and then sent on to New Orleans.
>
> Only God knows what will become of them. If you do not attend to the business, *all will be lost*. Mr. Turner says I must not speak on this subject, that if I do, it will weaken your claims to the property, which is what they are trying for. He says your claims are good, that they will stand good in law, but that *you* must attend to it. Either come yourself or empower some person to act for you. . . . If not . . . all will be lost, which indeed I cannot bear to think of. If you could only know how I feel you would try to take care for yourself. It is not for myself that I plead so hard. It is for yourself and your family.
>
> I . . . sincerely pity the negroes. They all flew to the woods at the sight of the Sheriff like wild hogs, and carried their little ones with them. . . . They returned only when he was safely gone.
>
> *Poor little Isaac is one that is seized.* I wish I had sent him to you by Arthur or that I had never loved him as I do. He is the smartest little boy on the place by far. If you will save them from being sold to strangers, I will ask no more. If you wish to move them to your Island, I shall not say one word against your doing so, and if you think proper to let them remain here, I shall be happy in doing the best I can for you and them.

I believe it is 16 or 18 that are seized and perhaps the rest may be in like manner ere this reaches you.

I dare not mention the business to any living soul but Mr. Turner, fearing it might injure you. But indeed I have pleaded hard to him to save it for you.

She closed her appeal with an apology for writing such a letter, but her "heart was so sore" that she could not help it. So she went on appearing "indifferent as a fool," even to the sheriff—"poor me saying nothing."

In the weeks that followed, Arthur was on the road day and night carrying letters to and from David and Rachel and her lawyers in St. Francisville. All was "hurry and bustle," and Rachel's mind was "so tormented" about "David's business" that she "could scarcely sleep any." She had just sent Arthur on horseback to David's home with papers that Mr. Turner wanted Judge Bushnell of "Iber Ville" to sign. This was so important that, in spite of Clarissa being very ill, she had persuaded Mr. Davis, Clarissa's husband, to join them in Iberville Parish. The situation was desperate and there was no time to lose. So "rain or shine" she hoped David himself might also be there. She, too, would gladly go if she thought she could render any service.

All this was part of the lawyer's moves to check the Flower brothers and to protect Rachel and David from future raids. The first step was to sue the securities, sheriffs, and all concerned for damages. As far as Rachel could learn, her "enemies were now much frightened" and one Courtney had sent word that he was coming to see her on business. Just now, she said, "he might as well stay away," for she would say nothing to him. The tide was turning in her favor and silence was wisdom.

For the present, at least, her attention could turn to the terrible cholera epidemic, which was sweeping across Louisiana, and to Mr. Mulkey, whom she had just rehired for the coming year "at six hundred dollars and to find his family in meal, and feed his riding horses." He was a sober man, she said, and understood planting as well as any other she knew. Some might think that all overseers were alike, but she knew better. Few could get the hands to do as much work as Mulkey could and he did not appear to abuse the Negroes or to have wives amongst them. She added as an afterthought the words "so far."

She then wrote her brother that the cotton bales were still at home because the sheriff had refused to "let them be sent to market." She was, however, not allowed to mention anything about business to anyone. She must still not show the least interest on any account.

That did not include the cholera. She still feared that every day might be her last. The news from New Orleans "up the Mississippi" was that the disease was still raging. Clarissa would soon be well if she were not frightened to death on hearing how bad the cholera was and had been. Among Rachel's papers can be found a detailed description of the disease and "a mode of treatment recommended by a gentleman." The best, however, was her own—not to let her Negroes go near the town "or any other place." She had ordered them to let her know the moment they felt unwell and not to pretend to be sick when they were not. A neighbor had gone even further. He had fenced up the lane to his house and written on a paper pasted to a post at the end of the property: "Friends and Foes pass by!"

Yet one good thing might come from the cholera. There would probably be no court session the coming December. That, however, did not just now improve Rachel's health. "If I could sleep at night," she said, "it would rest me greatly but among other distresses that blessing is denied me." Even when she fell asleep, dreadful dreams awakened her. Deaths, she said, were so common in St. Francisville that she would not allow any of her people to go there regardless of how pressing the business.

As to other matters, she was pleased to hear from Mr. Turner that the Flowers' lawyer had told him that they had made a great mistake in bringing the levy on the Negroes and that he, this lawyer, had about made up his mind to throw over the whole business. Even William Flower said that they "had overreached themselves" and that he did not know what the consequences might be. Mr. Turner was delighted and declared that nothing better could have happened.

As the last month of 1832 began, Rachel confessed to being almost tired of herself were she not afraid to die. She was desperately ill and the doctor so uncommonly attentive that she knew he thought her in danger. As she slowly mended after three weeks in bed, she was so weak that she could "set up" only a few hours each day. She was, however, feeling much better and confident that she would soon regain her health. Mr. Davis, Clarissa's husband, had been with her recently, and she was certain that Clarissa could not "be sensible of the blessing kind heaven" had bestowed on her in a husband or she would be more careful of her own health.

Charlotte and her son were in good health, and she had set her heart on returning to live on the old Swayze homestead. Henry Flower's suits on the estate and on Rachel, however, stood in the way, and Charlotte had at last given up with a broken heart, to Rachel's sorrow.

As her health returned, Rachel's attention was more and more required by plantation matters. On the day she had taken sick there had been words between her and Mulkey about some corn that had been left in the field, and she had told him he could go whenever he wished. He appeared, she said, "to be much raised," and she was afraid he wanted to be a great man. He had done better since their trouble and was getting the logs ready to roll where Patrick had cleared. "He understands farming very well," she said, "but he has trouble with the truth. He would seldom tell the truth if he could avoid it. He would even tell stories on the negroes when angry with them," but she hoped he would *manage to raise one good crop.*

She noted that David had recently sent for her care some valuable racehorses. They were beautiful animals, sensitive, and the older one cross at times, but both looked like they could "fly." Several people had called to see them and praised them greatly. Mulkey was taking good care of them, and she found them looking better now than when she became sick.

As for herself, she was determined not to neglect her duty to David and his family. She would never "sit at ease" while William Flower and the sheriff carried off all of their property on this side of the Mississippi. She was determined to do anything and everything in her power to prevent it. Fighting this problem was a pleasure to her, and she could ride "Big Black" thirty miles, one day after another, with ease while she was frightened but, as soon as the crisis was over, old age returned, and she could not undergo more than half a mile.

David had also been busy. He had appealed the judgment by the Third District Court against Rachel and had brought suit in the Louisiana Supreme Court for damages against William Flower. Flower denied that David Weeks was in possession of the property seized, alleging that there was a simulated sale from his debtor Rachel O'Connor to her brother entered into collusively to defraud him. The property had always remained in Rachel's hands and was therefore subject to seizure. The jury voted against David, and his exceptions were rejected. Yet he had asserted his ownership of the property and his willingness to defend it. That was an important step.

4/ A Woman Planter, 1830-1836

On January 19, 1833, Rachel wrote her brother David that she had no cause to complain of Mr. Mulkey as an overseer. He was very industrious and well behaved and "confined himself more to the truth than usual." Since news of the cholera had died away, things had gone well on the plantation. She herself had, of late, discovered that cottonseed, if boiled, would make the cows give much more milk and was better food for the hogs as well. If David could send her a larger kettle, she could soon make butter enough to pay for it. Her guinea sows would soon have pigs, and she already had eighteen pretty lambs and nine calves not more than a month old. Meanwhile, "down in the quarters," Charity had had a fine daughter—just like Patrick. Then, to add to her satisfaction, Rachel had learned that the Flower brothers were having trouble selling the cotton they had seized. She hoped they were "paying up in kind" for the trouble they had caused her last fall.

All this, if put together, gives an adequate picture of life on Rachel's plantation as the new year got under way. Things were so quiet that for the first time in years she could indulge her feminine interests. So, on a March day when Mulkey could find no work for the children, she set them to carrying manure for the garden, which she in better days had planted and tended. It was a garden of flowers and flowering shrubs as well as of vegetables. It had been designed for both utility and beauty, an expression of a woman's touch in a man's world. The garden had lost something in the bitter days when Rachel was left alone, but her interest now stirred again, when her sister sent two leaves for her to identify and when time could be spared for a leisurely answer. Rachel's reply reveals a side of her that the necessity of dealing with overseers had more or less covered over:

> I think the two leaves that you enclose are both of one kind and that the bush is a *Perrywinkle*. I do not see that they resemble any other leaf in the garden. The *Perrywinkle* is a small evergreen vine that bears blue flowers, very pretty near pickets or small bushes on which they run up.
>
> The *Syringo* grows 10 to 12 feet high, looks more like a vine than a bush and needs something to support it, to keep it from bending and growing crooked. I have several planted in the same place with the *crape myrtle*, and twisted together which keeps the *Syringo* straight. The *Syringo* bears white flowers and are in bloom at this time. The *Crape Myrtle* blooms in June or July which nearly prevents a person from

observing that there are two kinds planted in one place. They both stand the cold weather without shading. The *Jerusalem Cherry* is a small ever-green bush that bears berries resembling plumbs, only full of seed like the red peppers. Sometimes the leaves get killed in very cold weather but they come from the root again; the *scarlet lights* grow like *Pinks* and bear seed in the same manner, and often live all winter. The *butter and eggs* never give out, the seed falls, and come up again, something like the *larkspur*. The plants will have to be thined. The *Autance* or *Hortance* is tender and to be planted in a box where it may be set in a shady place where the sun can not reach it during the summer, and covered from the front in the winter. The flower first appears a greenish white and in several days becomes a beautiful pink colour which lasts for several days. Sometimes, however, the flowers are blue. They are beautiful when they do well. If I live and have my health I hope to send you some flower seeds against another year. I was too sickly to save any for you last year. I have a small cutting of *yellow roses* that Charlotte send down for you. If it lives I will send it on next winter. Have you any of the flowering *ammon*? I can send you some of that also if you wish it.

She closed by saying that the girls were all well and that she was sorry to say that her brother and herself were sued again and that she had sent the papers on to Mr. Turner.

The feminine side of the planter again came to the surface when a salesman had his spinning machine sent out in Daniel's cart. The machine "done so well" when he set it going that she bought it for $140. This would force her to be very industrious to raise that amount of money, but the machine spun so beautifully that she thought it would ultimately save its price. She had, in fact, at first refused to buy it and had tried hard to keep herself from wanting it, but after seeing it work she lost the fortitude she had previously thought so firm. Now she was as bad off as before, for she could not get any cotton in the seed to spin until some was raised. Meanwhile she kept on trying to justify the purchase and to rationalize her action by talking of the help it would be in clothing the Negroes. Mulkey helped her by promising to build a new loom house after the crop was laid by. Arthur could then learn to weave and teach others. Yet she expected her relatives to be surprised and to laugh at her for getting into "such a working notion." In fact it appeared strange even to herself that she had let her "mind have its own way too much in counting chickens before they were hatched." But Rachel had her machine and the salesman had his money.

Successful as Rachel had become as the manager of a large plantation, there were times when she "recollected the cares of a mother and a wife" and sincerely wished that it had been in her power the day she had lost her younger son to have "abandoned and forsaken all freely" and to have become a member of her brother's family. Even now, if she had an overseer who could be trusted to do what he should do and to be honest, she would love to be with them a part of her time. But Patrick had failed her and Mulkey, if left to himself, would soon become a "great man," spoiling the Negroes and spending his time "at play and eating." It was her firm opinion that neither overseers nor slaves could be trusted. Recently, Mrs. Pirrie's "fine carpenter" had written passes and sold them at five dollars each to slaves in the neighborhood. Some of the slaves had run away and now the carpenter himself was gone.

In contrast, Rachel's own plantation was all quiet, and Mulkey was "*so far* doing extremely well." He was the smartest overseer that had ever managed the place and would raise the best crops. He had conquered the grass, and his corn looked beautiful. His sweet potatoes and cotton were just as fine. Then, to climax the good news, Harriet had just been delivered of a little daughter to "the great joy of Old Sampson" and, of course, of Rachel, who could assure David that one more had been added to his "stock of negroes" on the plantation.

The general situation, however, was not good and was getting worse. Some of Rachel's cotton had gotten to market but the sheriff had stepped in and checked the flow. More alarming was the widespread sickness of all kinds in every neighborhood. Louisiana was living up to its reputation along this line with unusual vengeance. The cholera was bad at the landing and several Negroes had died within a few days' time. Down at Rapides it was so bad that the planters were leaving their crops and camping out in the pinewoods with the Negroes that were yet alive.

Both Rachel and her slaves had been "seriously sick" much of late and without medical care because the doctors themselves were ill. As she put it, she had been very sick and continued to be "quite unwell" and scarcely able "to keep about." Mulkey said the fields were in fine shape but she had been too poorly to ride out to see them. Yet, when Mulkey allowed her to have Old Leah to "assist at spinning, and old Milly to weave," she suddenly felt better. It did not last long however and, on a short trip to be with Charlotte "at the time of her confinement," Rachel was taken very ill and had to be brought home in a carriage. On the way they were met by a Negro coming for her who said that fourteen of her slaves were dangerously sick. One of these was poor Old Daniel, her faithful market man. He was "upwards to sixty years" and very frail and, though Dr. Denny did all in his power, day and night, to save him and Rachel herself nursed him "as she would a child," he soon numbered among her dead. As she saw him carried to the little plantation graveyard, she wrote: "I can safely say I never lamented the death of a Negro, as I do his. He has long been very useful, and more faithful than any other negro will ever be to me. I never shall have the same confidence in another. I feel satisfied with my conduct towards him, still I lament his loss. The rest of the sick negroes are alive but a part very low. I never had so much sickness amongst the negroes before since I lived on the plantation. . . . I feel so discouraged that I am afraid that I shall not be able to bear up against my misfortunes, but I will do the best I can while I do live." Weeks later she said that her garden looked bad but, each time she started out to have some work done to make it look better, the moment she got outside she thought of Old Daniel and of all his work for such a long time, and she could not stay. Tears filled her eyes and the weeds had their way.

Rachel's concern over Brother David's ill health was even greater than over her own or that of "her people." It caused her mind to hang between hope and despair. She could not sleep well and her dreams were confused and unpleasant. He had been quite sick and had taken a sea trip to New York in hopes of improvement. He had consulted doctors there and had just returned home by way of the Tennessee Mountains. He looked and felt better. At this news Rachel was overjoyed and wrote that, since she had heard of *his* health being on the mend, *she* "had got quite well" herself and "was surprised to find" her strength returning so fast. Clarissa's comment was that Rachel's uneasiness was what had kept her so poorly.

Throughout the fall and winter of 1833, sickness and death dominated the news in Rachel's world. She had never known it to be so sickly. Seventeen of her own Negroes had been down at one time. Dear Old Daniel was dead and now Old Sampson was very ill. Even Mulkey had been very low and his entire family sick at one time. The "blacks and whites" in both East and West Feliciana parishes had been "dreadfully sick." News of John Swift's death and that of Judge Rhea's two daughters and wife had just come and with it the report that Captain James Williams and a Mrs. Week lay at the point of death, as did the entire McCaleb family. The whole neighborhood was in distress. The calls on Rachel for help were so constant that she could not find a half hour "to set." No wonder her correspondence was so far behind. Even as she wrote, word came that a small girl at Mr. Bronson's had just died. "God only knows what will become of us." The cholera had not come near this time but the bilious fever and bowel trouble were nearly as bad.

Sick or well, work on the plantation had to go on and plans made for the coming year. Mulkey was still very industrious and no person could complain of his management. The plantation needed some "slicking up" but that was due to so much sickness among the slaves. There was, however, for the first time, a note of dissatisfaction with Mulkey that came out clearly in her talks with his wife. Rachel admitted his ability to manage and direct a plantation. He understood farming as well as anyone she had ever known, but others were saying that he was like all overseers. *They could not bear good treatment.* She suggested that his wife tell him this.

A short time later as she was making her plans for the year, she wrote that she had hoped that Mulkey would behave better, but she was doubtful. "He is a shameless being, nearly as bad as Patrick in the same way." He had too many ladies to please. He was a smart overseer but a dirty beast after all. There would be a new overseer for the next year. A Mr. Germeny had applied and she was investigating his record.

She found Mr. Germeny recommended as a capable overseer, industrious, sober, and reasonable in his demands. He would come for $470, did not wish to keep a horse, and had no children or slaves. But what pleased Rachel most was that he had a wife whom he loved and no children. He was clear of the fault so common among overseers, and on one occasion he had even driven a valuable carpenter away for bad behavior of the usual kind. That was enough. Rachel hired him on the spot for the coming year.

But the present year was not ended and Mulkey was still the overseer. The atmosphere was already tense enough when Brother David asked Rachel to send some of her Negro boys down to a plantation near Baton Rouge to assist his wife's brother Alfred Conrad in cutting his sugarcane. Mulkey protested that it would be impossible to save his own crop if his labor force were depleted. Rachel for her part was so distracted that she was almost ready to refuse. Yet it was David, as owner, who had requested it, and a Mr. Wycoff had already arrived to carry out the project.

So Dave, Eben, Harry, Littleton, and Frank "started on board a steam boat from St. Francis Ville." They left behind a lone woman with deep, rich, human qualities pouring out her very soul on a piece of paper:

> There have been so many accidents happening to steam boats of late that my heart trembles for their safety. They are all young and have never been from home before farther

than where Mr. Lewis Davis lives, which caused the very
idea of being sent amongst strangers to frighten them almost
out of their senses. . . . I am so sorry for them and I am very
uneasy, fearing they may take the cholera and die. They have
all been very sick this season and might die with a slight
attack. They were born and raised here with me which causes
me to love them better than I ought, but my heart must remain as it pleased God to form it. I have no power to change
it, or make it otherwise. . . . Dave will be 23 years old the
last day of December next, the other four are younger. When
the boys are to return home, do let them walk. They can
come home in two days without risking their lives on water
and in fire. [I hope] that Mr. Conrad will send them home
the moment he can spare them.

Rachel's worries grew and deepened as her boys departed. She remembered that she had not made new coats
for them this fall. Their last winter ones were quite good,
and the warning had been so short that she had no time to
prepare clothes for them, as she would have liked to do.
But she had done the best she could on short notice. After
they had gone she became very uneasy at their being at the
sugar works without their new coats. So she "concluded"
to make each of them a warm blanket coat and send them
down by Arthur. At sunrise the next morning he was on
his way. Rachel had toiled all night. When he returned he
carried a letter from Mr. Conrad saying that Harry, Eben,
and Littleton had left him and undertaken to make their
way home. They had, however, been caught and lodged
in jail at Baton Rouge. Conrad had found them and taken
them back to his plantation, where since they had behaved
very well.

Rachel was alarmed and was certain that Mulkey had given them bad advice or they would never have thought of doing such a thing. Those boys were too young to have "undertaken the likes" unless encouraged by some person. Mulkey liked Dave and probably had advised him to behave well and, since Frank was so young, he of course remained with Dave. On the other hand, Eben had once caught Mulkey and Eliza together and told Mrs. Mulkey, which caused a great fuss. Being guilty, Mulkey could not whip Eben without Rachel's consent, which, of course, was not given. Furthermore, Rachel had confined "the young madam" to her room, whipped her, cut off her curls, and sent her to the field where she had remained ever since. So Mulkey had good reason to advise Eben and the others to run away and to get into trouble—at least Rachel thought that this was the case. She was more certain of it when she learned that Mulkey had rejoiced when he heard that the boys had been caught and whipped.

Regardless of his part in the present case, Rachel hated the wretch. He had been saying that money could not tempt him to oversee her plantation another year, which he knew was a lie. He was a first-rate hand to raise and work a crop, but he was "a triffling whelp at gathering it in as ever was. He is now making fun of Germeny" who, she was sure, could not be as mean as *he* was. So she was willing to let Mulkey leave even before the end of the year, for Germeny could come at any time now and would do better than this fellow was now doing. Perhaps she was a bit too hard on him, not wanting him around any longer, because she was vexed at his conduct. Patrick, bad as he was, never was half as bad as "this vilian." The one thing she wanted most was for her boys to return home, and she knew that Mulkey would rejoice at her disappointment and theirs if they did not.

So Mulkey left at the end of November and Germeny and his good wife came at once. Meanwhile Harry and Frank had come home. Frank looked bad and Harry only a bit less. They reported that Eben was very sick and had been left behind. So Arthur was immediately sent to bring him home by one means or another and Dave and Littleton were to be allowed to come with them. Mr. Conrad, however, ordered Arthur home without saying or writing one word in answer to her request. Rachel was deeply hurt, saying she would probably never again hear from her boys. They might even be dead, for a number on that plantation had recently died of cholera or something else. The overseer and driver there were the cruelest beings Rachel had ever "heard of." If her boys were dead, it was only fair to let her know. If they were alive, she needed them at home.

Then, to add to her troubles, poor Old Sampson had died early that morning after being sick only a few days. She had given him every attention possible but all was in vain. Her heart was sore, and she had no idea that his death could distress her so deeply. "I should have been much happier," she said, "if I had never owned any living thing"

—and that even included her horse Old Ball that had died recently.

To add to Rachel's troubles, Mulkey had deceived her regarding the cotton crop. He had kept up her hopes to the very last for a good yield. Instead there were only "a midling" eighty-four bales. She could not bear to see him should he come for his final pay. Her only consolation was that Germeny continued to be very industrious. He was careful of the corn and the horses and stayed at home all the time. At least her Negro boys were now back home. Harry and Frank had run away and returned first and then, ten or twelve days later, Dave and Littleton came "without leave" from Mr. Conrad. She was sorry they had come that way but she thought it useless to send them back—they might start home again. Only poor, sick Eben was left, so she "got Mr. Doherty to take a trip down aboard a Steam Boat and bring him back. He looked bad, but being home, soon brought him back to health." Rachel did not feel guilty for her part in what had happened, for they were fine boys and no overseer had ever complained of them here at home. Anyway she had not sent the "runaways" back for fear they might be shot "as runaways" on the way.

David evidently did not complain, so Rachel pressed him a little further and begged that the iron band that had been riveted around Lid's neck be removed. She felt sorry for her: "She was a good girl before that vilian came here, and I scarcely think that there is one negro woman in existance, that is not guilty of the same wickedness. They are poor ignorant beings, born to serve out their days, and are led astray by such vile wretches as Mulkey who, no doubt, will have to account, ere long, for the sin they have commited, and are the cause of being commited."

She then recalled how a little fourteen-year-old girl, recently "purchased and given" as a house servant to Charlotte, had mixed poison, kept to "kill rats, with the family sugar." Serious as the matter was, Rachel did not denounce the child, but only noted that none of *her* poor Negroes had ever shown any desire to take any person's life. She went on without a break in her thinking to say that Mrs. Young's son-in-law had forbidden Mulkey to come near or visit his Negro quarters at night and had threatened to whip him if he did.

So now with her boys at home and Mr. Germeny doing so well (he could not do otherwise, he was so attentive, staying with his hands while they worked, staying at home nights and Sundays continually), Rachel could relax. Only the bad weather and sickness were holding things back. The weather had been dreadfully wet and Germeny had been delayed with his work. He had, however, finally gotten his corn and cotton planted. Sickness had swept the quarters and both children and adults had been stricken. Rachel herself had been quite ill with pains in the breast, a matter that would be mentioned more frequently as time went on.

For the present, the important fact was that Brother

David was in serious condition again and was on his way north. Someone who had seen him in New Orleans had reported him very weak and wasted away to skin and bones. Rachel was a bit skeptical of the report but, regardless of its truth or falsity, she was so worried that she became quite sick for the next six or eight days, could not "set up," and was "stuned to her very heart." She scarcely knew whether she was feeling or not. Once before, in time of trial, she had written, "It is our duty to submit to the will of Providence which ought to be considered as soon as possible. Otherwise we may draw on ourselves double sorrows. The *later* I accuse myself of in times past. Had I been more resigned at first, I dont think that my misfortunes would have been so severe,—which, too late do I lament but still hope to be forgiven what I so or inconsiderately [have] done." She now wrote that, while she had ever thought it a duty to submit patiently, she now feared she would fail in this last trial. She had lost all her near relations, all her brothers and sisters, and borne it with fortitude until she faced the threat of this last and only brother being taken before her own last days. She could only pray that David's wife would not permit her sorrow to rob her little ones of a mother.

Her last letter from David had been filled with so much goodness, and her heart had become so full that she scarcely knew whether she was in existence or not. She would take care of his property as far as health permitted, but she feared that her sorrows were greater than old age could bear. Yet she knew that it was her duty to comfort others and to forget herself. Her garden, she added, had been so uncommonly good and would continue to be so if she only had any heart to pay attention to it.

The days that followed as she waited for news of David's condition were bitter and filled with fear. No news was almost as painful as bad news, and letters to and from David's wife provided little relief. Each tried to console the other and to hide her own real feelings. The interesting thing about Rachel's letters is the deep religious feeling that had not characterized her earlier expressions:

> I make my sorrows known only to my God and Pray for mercy and deliverance from guilt. Through faith in the atoning sacrifice of Christ my Savior my affections on earth have become habitual, but to think of an endless Eternity, distracts my Brains, when one disobedient act is sufficient to condemn a sinner and banish him from all precious promises of the gospel. O' that I had always felt as I now feel, if they had coveted my coat, they might have taken my cloak also rather than suffer in mind as I now do. I pray for all fervently. If all the creation could be worthy of Heaven and the Blessing of God it would meet my most earnest Prayers.
>
> I am glad to hear of your house girls behaving so well. I have no doubt of your being right in judging mean, low white men, being the chief cause of their disobedience. It is always the case where they are, they cause more punishment to be inflicted amongst the poor ignorant slaves than all else they commit otherwise. Any white man that encourages the likes are next to the old evil one in badness.

As time passed with no news of David, the strain was

more than Rachel could bear. She became so ill that she could not raise her head or let it be raised without fainting. She could not remember ever being so weak. Then came a brief note from Alfred Conrad saying that he and David had reached New Haven safely. In a few hours Rachel's fever disappeared and she was out to find that Mr. Germeny continued to be very good and industrious and had every appearance of a fine crop of both corn and cotton.

In haste she wrote to David "requesting him to wear flannel and to be very cautious of his diet" and then to his wife urging "her not to let her present distress affect her health." These were the letters of a noble woman who had known little but trouble herself in life, twice a widow, once as a young girl and again when a husband literally drank himself to death. Her sons had added little and were now gone. Only in the affection and help of Brother David did she find comfort. Now a letter from his brother-in-law Conrad, dated August 16, brought the sad news of David's rapid decline.

What that meant to Rachel can only be revealed in her own words written to Conrad:

> Miserable as I am I must try to write you a few lines. I received your letter dated the 16 of August, last evening. A more distressed, unhappy being never was, and I hope never may be while the world lasts than my poor unfortunate self. From your letter dated the 28 of July I raised great hopes. My beloved Brother had mended so much from the 22nd which was the date of your letter to Mr. Doherty. My God is able to raise him again I must hope, and trust in his mercy.

Should your next bring the fatal news of his being no more, this bruised heart of mine will break. I have borne up against many trials knowing it to be my duty to submit to the will of Providence but I am now too weak and far advanced in life to stand the loss of so dear and only Brother. I shall be left too much alone in the world to bear so great a loss. I have been sick nearly all the time since he started from home.

My best of friends Pray to God for me, ask all the good to Pray for me. My heart and head burn. I am distressed, abject indeed. Do write and let me know all. Unless I gain strength fast I shall scarcely be in a situation to leave home. . . . Dont return by sea. Storms are very often at this season. The river is the safest. . . . Dear friend I sincerely Pray that you may never feel as I do at this period. I never felt as I do now. God only knows what is to become of me. Most willingly could I lay at the feet of all those kind friends that have attended on my beloved and kind brother and wash them with my tears, and I could find a plenty, they flow freely, but could I shed rivers of them they would not be too much.

Then the final news and a long silence.

5/ In the Shadows, 1834-1840

The death of Brother David in far-off New England, on August 25, 1834, marked the end of another period in Rachel O'Connor's life. In a broader sense it also marked the end of the era that had produced her. The agricultural frontier had already yielded to the new day of great planters, great fortunes, great houses, and great parcels of slaves. Louisiana like the rest of the South had begun drifting unknowingly toward civil war.

Stunned and overwhelmed by her brother's death, poor Rachel wrote that she was too far advanced in life to expect comfort in this world. Only the kindness of the best of brothers and that of his good wife had kept her alive after meeting the many afflictions that had fallen to her lot. She now feared that David's death would prove too great a loss ever to be borne. His kindness had prevented her from complaining. Now that he had been taken away she could no longer forbear complaint. He was the last and she loved him better than all that had gone before. She had placed her all on him and seldom grieved for those who had been taken long since. Now she was forced to think of them, too, and to grieve for them all.

Yet the plantation was still there and was to be her home under her own management as long as she lived. That had been David's promise. It was now late October. The cotton that had been picked during the recent rainy spell had turned yellow but that being picked now was beautiful. She had sixty-five bales pressed and ten or twelve ready to press. She hoped for at least ninety bales altogether. Her corn had also turned out well, and there was nearly enough for the coming year. She had kept as busy as possible for, when she stopped and thought of her troubles, she "must cry without ceasing." Her spirits were low. Daily did she lament her many sad and grievous misfortunes. She could pray for every soul that lived and wish them never to experience the different sensations that had fallen to her lot. She hastened to add that, since it had been the will of her Heavenly Father to place her on earth, it might also be His pleasure to guide her through life. "We must submit to the will of Providence and had ought to do so without a murmur. Knowing all is just and right that is done by Him that cannot err."

This turning to religion and constant willingness to accept misfortune as the will of God soon found expression in Rachel's being baptized "at residence" and confirmed at

Grace Episcopal Church by Bishop Leonidas Polk. At the same time she had all her slaves baptized, a fact that she nowhere mentioned in correspondence with her closest relatives.

Perhaps her occupation with the life to come was made possible by the conscientious care with which Germeny managed the mundane affairs of the plantation. Over and over again she praised his work and his behavior. "Mr. Germeny," she said, "has conducted so well in every respect that" she "sincerely thought that his honest and honorable behavior deserved nothing but praise." He was far from putting himself on a footing with those under his charge. He had no favorite misses to fight and abuse the boys about, so all went on as it should. Germeny was the only man who had ever overseen her plantation who was "clear of that weakness." Even when feeling "poorly," he was never "laid up." He was an honest man and his word could be depended on. She summed it all up by saying that he was the first overseer she had *ever* liked in *every* respect. Most others had been "meaner than mean itself."

Perhaps Dr. Denny and Lawyer Turner also served to add a bit of "unexpected comfort" to Rachel's stay in "this world." She was soon feeling more in debt to Dr. Denny than ever before. Her Negroes had been unusually sickly and he had given them, even while she was away, the best of attention. He had, at Rachel's request, gone up north to attend Clarissa and had remained several days until she was out of danger. He would be at Rachel's bedside a few years later when death came and would witness her last will and testament. Lawyer Turner gave legal advice, standing between her and the Flower brothers when they threatened her property. Well might she say that she had no idea that she still had so many sincere friends.

In spite of Rachel's feeling that she was not long for this world and her hope that no other person ever had, or might have, such feelings as tortured her hourly, she was in fact slowly finding her way back into the stream of everyday affairs. It was not a Rachel thinking of the golden streets above who asked for twenty-eight yards of cheap calico, and "please to let it be gay," to make a dress for every woman who bore her a Negro child. She was now in debt to four who had young babies "and fine ones too." She commented, "They do much better by being encouraged a little," and she had "ever thought they deserved it." She would also like for the slaves fifteen bed blankets, which might be cheaper in the spring than in the fall. She would also like for the calves to run with the cows until the pasture improved. She slipped back a little when she hoped that the crop would prove more than good, but if it should please God not to grant her wishes she would try to make it up by taking care of what was here, which had always been the way that the greater part of her property had been collected together.

How firmly Rachel still held to the frontier attitude toward acquiring and holding land and rounding out a plantation came out in her constant effort to buy every bit of land on her border as it came onto the market. She noted in June, 1835, that Mr. Weems had offered his plantation of four hundred acres for only four thousand dollars. She urged Alfred Conrad, who was now looking after his sister's business affairs, to come to an agreement with the owner, for the land would add much to their plantation and could be paid for easily without missing the amount due, because of the length of time permitted to make the payments.

That opportunity was missed but, when in October some neighboring land was to be sold at public auction, she asked, "as a particular favor," which she hoped and prayed might be complied with, that she be allowed "to buy it in." The purchase would add greatly to the estate and to the convenience of the plantation. She knew that Brother David had intended to place that power of purchase in her hands, because he had feared that some other person might keep the land should it sell cheap, but he had forgotten to have it done. At her death, she said, this addition would pay well for the money given and perhaps long before then in cropping. She had been sadly disappointed in missing the previous sale of land, which had already doubled in value. Her only desire was to manage for the best in the time she had to live and to add more land to the place, for land values would be higher every year anywhere near "St. Francis Ville." Mr. Conrad agreed to the purchase, provided of course that it could be had at its value. That satisfied Rachel and brought her a bit more "unexpected comfort" in this world. She, in turn, hoped that kind heaven would reward him for his goodness.

Widespread sickness, the infirmities of old age, and the problems of a society based on Negro slavery were, however, matters that could not, just now, be left to "Kind Heaven." Her dear Clarissa was "laying extremely low" and there had been little hope of her being spared during the past week. They had sent for Rachel to come but she herself was too ill to go. She had, however, sent word that, if Clarissa should be taken from this world of sorrow at this time, Rachel would soon be with her. Fortunately both were soon better. Yet Rachel insisted that she was not long for this world unless a great change should take place. She was so weak that a few moments of walking tired her and threw her into a fever instantly. That so exhausted what little patience she had left that in her dreams she would call out for her mother to come to her but, alas, she had no parents to comfort her in her sorrows. Even if she did have, they would perhaps be tired of her. In fact, she was tired of herself but still hoped and prayed that the world would bear with her a little longer.

It had been uncommonly sickly of late and a great number of persons, black and white, children and adults, had died and many now "lay at the point of death." Her Negroes were all alive but some had been very sick. Her nearest and dearest neighbor Mr. Bowman had just died, and she had limited her calls on his widow, whose grief

would soon have broken her own heart—that is, if she had
had any heart left to break. Sickness among her relatives
had left Rachel almost without company. Little Isaac alone
kept her in talk, otherwise she would forget how. Just
now, however, she was too ill for either talk or company.
She was scarcely able to move about the house. Rachel, like
the rest of Louisiana, was paying the price required for
living in a "Fertile Mud Paradise."

There were things other than sickness just now to dis-
turb the community. Wild rumors of slave uprisings and
the hangings of white men who were responsible filled the
newspapers. The whole region was supposedly full of
Murrell men, who made a business of stealing slaves, stirring up rebellion, and planning a great Negro insurrection
covering the whole Southwest. Highways were no longer
safe and the planters, in alarm, were organizing night
patrols for protection. The seizure and hanging of suspects
had reached the point where Rachel suggested that "we
should be careful of the children otherwise the world
might be left without people."

In her own community "the gentlemen of the Parish
had concluded to raise money by subscription to hire a
company of men to ride day and night as a guard over all
the Parish." Some had subscribed sums ranging from
twenty to one hundred dollars. Others had agreed to pay
twenty-five cents for each slave they owned, but Rachel
could not do so without Mr. Conrad's consent. Anyway,

she was not uneasy. She had raised her Negroes "better than to have such principles." She knew that mean white men were the cause of it all. Of the blacks in her community, not one had been found guilty of any bad act, while white men were being taken up on all occasions. There was one in jail just now who was expected to hang, which was more merciful than the common practice of whipping nearly to death, called "Linch Law," and then letting the suspects go with orders to be out of the state in eight hours.

Then to climax the whole situation, the "hard times" that had been building up through the past few years reached its peak in what was later called the panic of 1837. "I never knew the complaint so general before," Rachel wrote. "The Rich appear to be as much distressed as the poor, and all in want." Even the weather stepped in to play its part with a long, dry, hot summer. It was more than her fragile constitution could bear. For the next six months and more her pen was still. She too took her place near death's door and only the skill of Dr. Denny kept her alive. Even as late as the end of the following March her hands trembled "like a leaf in the wind" and she could write only a few lines at a time.

The Negroes in the quarters suffered even more than the whites in their better houses. In late September Rachel lost her little Isaac, whom she loved so much. In deep sorrow she wrote, "I have not enjoyed a day of health since he left. I sincerely hope and Pray that his little spirit is at rest and that mine may join in like manner whenever it should be the will of Providence to call me from this earth."

Providence, however, was a little slow in its call and plantation affairs ever more pressing. The old ginhouse was almost falling down and a new one was necessary. The old gin itself had to be replaced. She was aware of the times being hard but she was spending money only for provisions and for the good of the plantation, which she considered her duty for the short time she had to live.

This consciousness of age and growing infirmity in no way weakened Rachel's determination to stay right where she was and to go on with the management of the plantation as long as she lived. She was that kind of woman. On one day she would say that her health had changed so often that she could not guess how it would be on the morrow. It might be her last. So she lived each day for itself. Then in almost the same breath she would report that the Negroes "were all well but one," that she had three fine little Negro babies, and that the plantation was in fine order, with nearly all the corn planted and the cotton ground nearly ready to plant.

It is also interesting to note that, although Germeny, her overseer, had retired at the end of the past year and had moved to Jackson, no new overseer had been employed. Rachel and one of her Negro boys were carrying on alone. She was much elated when Germeny returned for a visit and discovered how well she had gotten along without him. She was, however, saddened by his frail appearance and subsequent illness while still at her home. He could walk only a few steps at a time and soon not at all. Even Dr. Denny's skill could not save him, and he was soon "laid to rest" in the little plantation graveyard. His death left another empty place in Rachel's shrinking world.

Rachel's growing tendency to bring "this life" and the "life to come" and "this earth" and "the Heaven above" into her letters and her conversations was striking evidence of the profound changes taking place in the woman herself. Even a young niece was told that death must come and we could not know the time. She must also learn that obedience to parents was the only promise in the Ten Commandments of a long life and that, if a parent ever experienced anything heavenly on earth, it was from dutiful children. Rachel prayed that goodness might guide all the children, step by step, to the place where all sorrow ends.

This was not the Rachel who had dared to build a cotton plantation in a man's world. It was an old woman who spoke of the "nothingness" in earthly gain and who looked forward to a better world in the life to come when her time in this one ended. Times had become hard for her and she lived in troubles day and night. She ended most of her promises with the statement "if I live that long" or "I trust in God who does all things well."

She followed these pious words with the information that this very morning she had the good luck of Charity being delivered of a fine daughter, who was likely to do well, for which she returned many thanks to kind Providence. This made five babies in recent months and all growing fine, but that did not make up for the loss of her poor little Isaac.

This emphasis on heaven and death mingled with the immediate worldly affairs was not just an emotional expression or even a compliance with the general trends of the day. It was, in Rachel's case, the sincere expression of a realist. She knew that she was old and frail and sick. She had already lived her allotted years, but she was the manager of a plantation and the owner of some eighty or more slaves, most of whom had been born on the plantation and between whom and herself was a loyalty deeper than usually went with slavery. She had raised them well and affection was not just on one side.

Impending death and the obligations of a planter to a plantation that was both a home and a trust presented quite a tangle. Under such conditions heaven and everyday affairs were, indeed, not very far apart. How true this was came out in a letter that Rachel sent to David's widow in early September of 1840. She spoke of her misfortunes, of the deaths of Ellen, twenty-two years old, Amy, three, Henrietta, one, and Old Sam of indefinite age. All these she had borne with great fortitude, but now her heart was nearly broken. She had lost poor Leven, one of the most faithful black men who ever lived. He was true and honest and without a fault that she had ever discovered. He had "overseed" the plantation for nearly three years and had done much better than any white man had ever done. She had, for the first time, been able to live a quiet life.

Leven had died in the early part of the night of August 27 and was followed, a few hours later, by his little daughter Clarissa. They were buried together and no pen could tell the distress Rachel felt. She hoped the Lord would be merciful to her or otherwise she must sink with grief. Six weeks later she wrote again saying: "I feel heart broken at the loss of Leven. I never knew so good a black man. I think that I may say with safety that he was without a fault. All my neighbors say the same and lament my loss. I have not been sick since he died but find myself much weaker and so discouraged that my time passes sorrowfully." She could not write about him without crying.

The sickness that had taken Leven had been widespread throughout the plantation and the neighborhood. Rachel had from ten to sixteen "laid up" for more than two months. A little girl fourteen years of age had lain speechless for all that time, while Nancy and Celest had been lingering at the point of death. Since the last of January seven of her Negroes had died, including "poor little Willis." Dave, Littleton, and Frank were all down at one time and Eben had been confined to his bed for nearly three months. So distressed was Rachel that she sent for the Reverend Mr. Lewis to come pray for her. He had come and had promised to come again.

Rachel's neighbors had fared no better. Sickness and death were all around the community. Scarcely any place had escaped. Homes as well as quarters had suffered. It was indeed, as Rachel said, "a general time of distress." In many places the worms had destroyed the cotton and the storms had been equally bad, but "kind Providence" had mercifully spared her plantation and only the sickness of her slaves had held things back. Poor Leven had left a promising crop and, if the hands would ever get able to work, she would try, under Arthur as overseer, to gather it in.

In Rachel's few remaining years she was, as she said, "never clear of trouble." She had not "laid up" one day for months. Her time was given to nursing the sick among her Negroes. Some had died and the loss of her little ones, along with Leven, had nearly broken her heart. No pen, she said, could convey her distresses. Mrs. Bowman had lost nine this summer and fall, which appeared not to cost her a thought. "Why cannot I be so," was Rachel's only comment. On another occasion, she had given the answer: God had not made her that way.

She revealed a bit more of the new Rachel when she explained to her niece why she had not written sooner. "I cannot write now as I used to do by candle light. I have so much to look after all day that I scarcely can spare the time to write. You are young now and know very little of the troubles of the world. You can at any time spare the time to write, if other amusements do not prevent. Youth is the time to enjoy life, after that passes off, and the cares of the world commence, we see very little but distresses."

Perhaps Rachel's most revealing statement made in these troubled days, when old age dominated, had to do with her reluctance to leave home for any length of time because she feared she might not be able to return. Her good, comfortable, old home was so precious that, when her time came, she wanted to die there. Others might not think that way, but no other place could ever be home for her. In this statement there was a hint that there had been some effort by David's heirs to gain possession of the plantation. Perhaps the income from Rachel's management had not been satisfactory. More probable was the fact that, as the family disintegrated, they were dividing up and parceling out their holdings. At any rate, it gave Rachel a chance to state her case.

The past two years had been difficult. Sickness and even death had swept through the quarters and her time had been largely given to the care of the stricken ones. She had done without a white overseer and had shared that position with a Negro boy. Yet she had planted, cultivated, and harvested her cotton crop and had sent to market a normal number of bales. She had also raised the usual amount of corn and potatoes. She had, moreover, torn down the old, dilapidated outhouses and replaced them with new structures. She had purchased the tar and iron needed and had hired a neighbor's blacksmith, who had cost less than if she had had the work done on the outside. She had built a new ginhouse and purchased and paid for a new gin. She was now ordering the cloth to make winter clothing and was asking that it be sent before cold weather set in, so she could get her part done early. Cold weather always brought pain to her poor, old bones, so she had to pick her time and get along by degrees as she was able. In other words, she was really as saving in every respect as she knew how to be. When her account would be called for by the Great Giver of All Good, she hoped to be found faithful in all things as far as she had known.

In a letter to Mr. Magill, who now represented David's heirs, she spoke her mind. There were some things, regardless of criticism, that she must do. She had not sent for "one barrel of pork for the Negroes to live on" or anything else toward their support, which he should know was not doing either them or herself justice. She was, however, willing to do almost anything for peace's sake. It was, however, out of all reason to expect a crop to be raised without "Provisions to feed the negroes on." As for herself, she could make less do her than almost any other living person were it not for the people saying so much about it all, knowing that she *had* served and *still served* her days faithfully and ought to have a peaceable and quiet life in her old age.

She asked for an immediate reply, for she must know what she must do "to rub through this year," should she live that long. Times were hard with her now and she lived in trouble day and night. She certainly hoped that, after her time on earth was over, she would be taken to a happier world. She asked only one favor. She would like to continue sending her cotton to the same brokers she had always found to be fair and helpful. If she could not choose her brokers she would be less than a common overseer. She would have Mr. Magill know that she had in her brother's own handwriting the acknowledgment that she was entitled to anything that she might want for herself or for the use of the plantation during her life. It was her frank opinion that David's heirs should feel pleasure in fulfilling their good father's desires.

Unfair criticism was not all that troubled Rachel just now; her hearing was nearly lost. She found it difficult to understand anything that was said. It was, she thought, a great punishment, but God's will must be done and she hoped that the time would come when she would find that it was good for her to be afflicted. She tried hard to feel resigned to fate but somehow she still mourned the loss of all of her family and missed her hearing. Neither prevented her from getting up early each morning, attending to her business, and getting along very well. She had not hired an overseer for several years and found the place much improved by not having any. She still had a good garden and found it to be a great help, especially in feeding the little ones. It took "a great deal" to feed so many, but it was her greatest pleasure to take care of them and to see them looking well.

Rachel's troubles with Brother David's heirs did not end abruptly. It was a period of change on all levels. The nation as a whole was moving out of the period of panic and depression. David's widow had become the wife of Judge John Moore, and her children were establishing homes of their own. Rachel's plantation might well be liquidated to their advantage. A letter from her nephew William Weeks had said something about Mr. Magill's alarm at her attitude toward the plantation. "I am greatly surprised," she said. "Your Poor Father was perfectly pleased with all he had done and with all that Judge Dawson had done." He had charged her against signing any papers respecting their business and urged her to take care of herself. So nothing would ever induce her to sign another paper.

I must have a home. I am too old now to go about like a wandering Jew. I never received one dollar in payment for the property. I had some notes on your father but have given them to your mother for his children. . . . I only wanted to live. Your father willed me the property during my life which was enough for me and after my death it belongs to his family. They have had all that I could make, excepting the support that the plantation and the negroes required. You are very young but do you really think that I should turn myself out of House and Home, at this age. I don't think that Mr. Magill would like to see his old mother turn herself adrift in that way, but be that as it may, I now declare that I will not sign one more paper. I cannot part from my Negroes. I have raised all but a few and I love them. They have their faults, and I have mine. All the living have faults, none are clear of sin. . . . I must be merciful to find mercy; I must forgive in the hope of being forgiven.

If your poor father were alive he would not wish me to be tormented, not for ten times as much as is here. He knew too well how to make a living for his family to wish to take any advantage of a poor deaf widow woman.

Rachel's letter had the desired effect. Young William stumbled back with an apologetic reply, which gave her a chance to further drive home her points. "You will not see as you do now," she replied, "if you live fifty years longer, which will bring you to the age of myself at this time. . . . The treatment I have received from numbers since I arrived . . . at fifty has caused me to fear my own shadow." Until then, she said, all the heirs had been satisfied with what she had done and had shown complete confidence in her. His letter, however, had caused her to fear that some person was trying to lead their young minds astray. She, therefore, wanted them all to understand that all business of all kinds had been done in the name and for the estate of Brother David and never in her own. She had acted only as an agent for the estate, which at her death would belong to the heirs. "Now my dear son," she added, "I think [the above] is sufficient to Prove that I do not consider this Property now with me as belonging to myself but lent to me by your Dear Father and to be supported from it during my life time and after my Death it belongs to his heirs."

How deeply Rachel felt about the threat to her plantation came out later when she looked over her fields, found them in "first rate order"—the corn up, the cotton being planted, and her new orchard now almost an idol.

I am afraid that I think too much of it all, and that God will punish me for letting my Heart cling to earthly treasures. I am not afraid to love the little black children. Christ suffered on the Cross for us all and it is my duty to take care of all that He has seen proper to place under my charge for His sake, which I do and love to do,—their mothers were all raised under my care. . . . It is love for the place and the people on it that causes all my earthly troubles. The name of riches has no value with me. That has long since been buried in the graves with my relatives and friends, but God is all love and has placed love in my heart for all,—particularly such as his just judgment placed under my care and given me a willing mind to do my duty in all things. So far as I know I have long since been nothing but a trouble to my friends. But I am what I am and must do what I do. I ask only for mercy.

I am tired.

6/ Evening, 1840-1846

Rachel was indeed tired. Sickness and old age had taken their tolls. She had, as usual, been very busy getting the crops planted in spite of having been confined to her bed for the past three weeks with violent pains in her back. She had been so ill that she could not rise, turn, or suffer anyone to assist her. She was better now but still far from being well.

"Times are hard with me now," she wrote. "I live in trouble day and night." She hoped that after her time on earth was over she would be taken to a happier world where all sorrow ends. Just now, however, plantation affairs kept her busy right here on earth. There was a fine chance of little Negroes coming on and, should blessing continue to attend them, they would assist greatly in a few years. Just now she had sixteen little ones, the oldest only six years of age. They were all healthy and, while her little favorite was lean and thin, he also seemed to be fine and healthy.

Then there was the task of securing supplies of every kind for "her people." Prices were so high that she was afraid she would be criticized. But she could not do on less. As she later wrote, she was as saving in every respect as she knew how to be, so that when her account would be called by the Great Giver of All Good she would be found faithful as far as she had known. Even when she had been so ill that Dr. Denny had called in another doctor, whose bill was sixty-one dollars, she could say this was all she had cost the estate in a year's time.

Just now Rachel's neighborhood was troubled by a rash of runaway slaves. One had been shot near Rachel's home. Nine had run away from "Daniel Turnbill's" [Turnbull?] plantation just down the road, but Rachel's plantation was going on as usual. Her slaves were quiet and industrious.

It is an interesting fact that, although Rachel was a rather large slaveholder, she had never had either runaways or uprisings. Her human kindness and devotion to the well-being of her slaves as individuals had seemingly made them view her somewhat as a friend engaged with them in a common enterprise. As the years went by, she had more and more disliked the institution of slavery and thought of herself as burdened by responsibility. She praised the Negro boys who took over when the overseers departed and pronounced them superior to any white man who had ever been on her place. She praised the Negro girls who stayed with her day and night when she was ill. They had remained at her side even when sick themselves and when no white woman was about. "I have every reason to be thankful to my God for all his goodness in opening the hearts of these women about the house to be so very attentive to me," was Rachel's strange comment.

Meanwhile, she found great comfort in recalling the fact that her house, a modest plantation structure, was "all mended up and repaired, with a new frame kitchen added, the yard all pailed in, and all very comfortable." She was certain that she would soon be able to resume her regular duties.

Rachel's garden looked bad. She had not been able to walk that far for weeks. In fact she was inclined to blame her garden for her sickness. The peas and beans and beets had been in such abundance and the weather so fine that she had not been able to keep away. She had been out there from morning to night, without once thinking of her old age. Her old back, however, had been conscious of the burden, and three weeks in bed was the price.

Other more serious things were also pressing home the bitter fact of rapidly passing time and its cost. In spite of all the deaf remedies that she and her friends had been collecting through the years, Rachel's hearing had grown steadily worse. She could scarcely understand anything that was said to her. All had to be written, so she had gotten a small slate for that purpose. As she said regarding a promised visit of friends, "I can only see them . . .

but my little slate is whole yet." She could at least try to have a good garden for them to see if they came later and she would be spared that long. She was, she said, much fallen away and so weak she could not write long at a time. She tired easily.

Added to her own troubles was the sickness and death of Clarissa's husband Lewis Davis. He had been her favorite from the time he came courting, and she regarded him as one of the finest young men she had ever known. "I loved him dearly," she said. "I feel as if I had lost another son. He has ever been kind to me." Young Davis had indeed been kind to Rachel. Even when "the girls" had been a bit withdrawn because of Rachel's leaving her property to David's heirs and ignoring them, Lewis had visited her regularly and had, on a few occasions when she was seriously ill, stayed several days to care for her. No wonder she could not get him off her mind. It is not surprising that she had not seen Clarissa since well before his sickness or that she remained cool in the days that followed.

That, however, did not matter so much just now, for after Brother David's death things had begun to assume a new and dangerous form. Alfred Conrad had suggested that Rachel retire and turn her plantation over to the estate. Rachel was stunned.

> God is my witness that I wish to act right, and since the arrival of your letter I have walked the garden with uplifted hands in fervent Prayer to my God laying my situation before

Him who knows all things, and on my knees with my face to the floor asked his assistance, Praying to be directed the way that is right. And now my dearly beloved friend I must ask yourself and my Sister to consider my unfortunate disposition of which my dearly beloved Brother was well aware and could have informed you, that to separate me from this plantation and the slaves on it would cause the remainder of my days to pass·off in deep sorrow.

If I could only be as many others in the world are, I would willingly sign anything you would think proper but as it is and to change the affair from what it was in the commencement would be in a manner consenting to my own misery and wretchedness. . . . I am at this period in the sixty-third year of my age and according to the course of nature shall not be a trouble to my friends much longer and must pray to them to bear the will of Providence patiently that Blessings may follow in return. I am alone in this world. My mothers children are all gone before me. I have none to ask advice of, neither have I asked any at any time.

Rachel closed by saying that her request, made some time ago, of having the property returned to her hands was owing to the idea that he, Mr. Conrad, was "discontented in some ways" with her management and disgusted with the attachment she felt toward the Negroes on the place. But she could not act otherwise, "after the care" she had taken to raise them and "the blessings the Lord of Heaven and Earth had bestowed in causing them to prosper under my care."

Her letter seems to have had the right effect, for nothing more, for the present at least, was said about signing papers or immediately giving up management of the plantation. In fact, Mr. Conrad went the full distance in the opposite direction. He urged her in case of need to draw on her cotton brokers for any amount of money she might need. It was, he said, impossible for him at his distance to anticipate her needs. Furthermore, his mind was occupied with his own business. He was new and inexperienced in planting and often vexed and worried out of his wits. So any apparent neglect of her affairs must be ignored. It was all due to his own confusion or his occupation with other pressing business. He had evidently learned a lesson.

In spite of all of Rachel's troubles, the love of her land and of her Negroes outweighed them all. She had seen her land turn from prairie to plantation and her babies from the cradle to servants and field hands. It had not been an easy road. As Rachel had written earlier: "We moved our little all to this place thirty-nine years ago and I have been serious all day trying to call to memory every act, thought, word and deed, during the thirty-nine years past, and have asked forgiveness for all faults and pray for all faults and pray for a blessing for the time to come and try every means to deserve it in my power." She closed by saying, "We came to this place in 1797 and it is wonderful to think-over all the misfortunes that I have lived through since that date and still fear death." Then unconsciously a mind, caught between the here and the hereafter, drifted to an overseer who cared for the corn and horses as if they were his own and to a neglected garden and to an old woman anxious to do her best as she always had done. Only gradually did her mind wander back to the starting point. Old age had its mental as well as its physical side.

After Rachel's serious illness of the past summer, her health seems to have improved somewhat. Only one thing caused serious alarm—a hard lump had developed on her right breast. It was "ugly looking" and very painful. Her mind was distressed, but up to now she had trusted in her God "who does all things well," and "if it were not for the best it would not be so." Dr. King, however, was of the opinion that it was not for the best. He pronounced it one of the worst kinds of tumors and, when it became so sore and painful that Rachel was ill, he thought it was time for *man* to step in and play his part. So, when Dr. Stone agreed with Dr. King that it was impossible to cure her breast and that an operation was necessary and when her nephew William Swayze joined them, she consented to let it be done. She was nearly scared to death as they cut away the diseased parts, but in the end as it began to heal she concluded that the Lord, after all, had been on the doctors' side.

It had, however, been an ordeal and she remained very weak. Her girls, Charlotte and Clarissa, now became exceedingly kind, and "Poor Charity and Fanny" had stayed by her day and night during her sickness and distress. She felt as if these two Negro girls were a part of herself from their goodness to her—"it must have been ordered by my God himself."

Rachel's health improved slowly and she would walk about her garden every morning and evening, trying to gain some strength. She had been "greatly afflicted" and had never expected to be able again to write a letter or to take care of the plantation. Her good neighbor William Hargadine had hired an overseer for her who had, "so far," done very well. He was "a midling old man," quite industrious, and had gotten along well with the Negroes. He was a "whimsical being" and had to be humored like a child. This she did not mind as long as he tended to his business. Furthermore, he was too old to be visiting the quarters at night.

This hiring of an overseer after her slave Arthur had served for three years, doing better than any white overseer had ever done, brought from Rachel some interesting comments. In the first place, overseers were expensive with their wives and children and sometimes with a horse to support. They were all alike in their morals and most of them, when given control over land, crops, and slaves, soon became "great people." Germeny had behaved very well for two years, but during his last two years he had been no better than the others. While her health was good she got along well, but when she was sick the white overseer soon learned how to take every advantage. Of all the beings on the earth, she thought the least of a white overseer. In this connection it should be added that her new overseer lasted only a short time. He was an excellent manager on a farm, but "as deceitful as sin." Rachel was really sorry to discover so much meanness in a being with a white skin.

Throughout the summer and fall after Rachel's operation, it became more and more apparent that she was losing ground. She spoke often of doing things "if I live long enough and my strength returns." She had been very sick most of the time with a high fever, which affected her "poor weak head" and caused her to be uncertain about what she had or had not done. She could sit up only for short periods, and for the first time there crept into her letters some question of her ability to go on managing the plantation. Her nephew William Weeks had advised her how to act respecting the money now held by Mr. Thompson—a member of the firm through which Rachel had always sold her cotton—but she hesitated to attempt any further business for fear of making some mistakes. She only wanted enough secured to her to supply the wants of the plantation and the Negroes on it. There was such "a fine parcel of fine looking little children" and her heart's only desire was to take care of them. She already had both the young and the old well clothed for the winter, but William's brother Alfred C. Weeks must come soon to assist in getting all other business done right. She could not do it alone.

It was her nephew Alfred on whom Rachel relied most for help now. As a young boy, he was considered wild, but now she thought of him as "a most gentle and charm-

ing youth." Rachel wrote: "I am at a loss of words to be-
stow praise equal to his goodness. I entertain no fear of
his being one among the best. He is very young to have so
much good sense."

His mother had once thought of sending him with her
other children to the North to finish his education. She
feared that he might unfortunately fall into bad company
in Louisiana. "I know but little about Baton Rouge," she
wrote, "but I fear Jackson will cause many a mother The
Heart ache. There are a number of good people living there
and as many far from being so good." Happily she kept her
children home, and Alfred had become Rachel's most
trusted relative.

A better indication of Rachel's fear of impending death
was the preparation of a list of her Negro slaves, which
she sent via Alfred to David's widow, now Mrs. Moore.
The list is long and detailed; it is given below only in
part. With motherly pride she grouped her families,
named the parents and the children, and noted their personal characteristics and the services rendered through past
years by the many. True, most of the large planters kept
full records, but there are few documents that reveal as
much information about the master and the slave as Rachel
crowded into hers. It is in fact a gentle woman's prayer
for those she loved but whom she must leave to the care of
others. The list tells as much about Rachel as it does about
her slaves. It is an autobiography unintentional. It reads:

I send to you by your son and my beloved Nephew Alfred
C. Weeks a list of negroes names and the family they come

of, which I Pray you and your sons to take care of for my sake after I am in my grave—Charity is a yellow woman born the 25th day of December 1812—she is a grand daughter of old Daniel and Leah and a daughter of old yellow George and Henny. Henny was a daughter of the above named Daniel and Leah, and a sister of Arthur's the present Drover. She has ever since her birth been a good girl but I did not know her worth until since my severe spell of sickness in July and August 1841, since that time I trusted her in all my House-keeping affairs. In the first instance my low state of health and weakness obliged me to do so and from finding her so very honest during that time, I have continued to trust her and as yet she has not shewed any wish to deceive me—I love her as a mother loves her good child—Pray, Pray my beloved friends dont let her and her children fall into cruel hands. She has five daughters, Viz, Nancy, Margaret, Frances, Mary, and Elizabeth and Perhaps may have another in 6 or 7 months from this time; old Patience has been my cook for thirty eight years the only one I ever had. I expect she is now sixty years old at least, but I Pray you be kind to her for the good she has done, she has five daughters the oldest have children and grand children. Pray do the best you can for all of old Patience's children and grand children—Eben is Fanny's husband. Harry and Songy are old Patiences sons. Songy is the best disposed and his wife Hetty is a fine girl. She was born the 30th of July 1828. She is sister to Charity. Eben is truly a good man and very trusty. He was born the 26 of Janry 1812. Arthur is a good slave and valuable, either 43 or 44 years old. We bought him with his father and mother old Leah's youngest son. I expect his mother is nearly seventy years old and Poor old Milly eighty five or six, please to have them taken care of, for the good they have done, they have served their time faithfully and are doing good yet. They were all born mine or here with me and raised chiefly in House with me while small.

Rachel followed this appeal with the names of all her slaves and their birth dates. She wrote:

> You will find that there are only sixteen men, the four that are first on the list were not born here on this place, all the rest of the males were—and there are eighteen women that are young enough to be good hands, the oldest of the 18 is 47 years old—and Hetty the youngest is 16 on July 30—Rhoda and Rose about two years younger and Nancy three years which makes 21 in all and two little boys Henry and John. Patience cooks for me, Old Milly raises Poultry, Old Leah spins wool, old Dinah is nearly blind but churns and feeds the cows and helps about all she can see to do. Charity is washer and attends about the house. I have a large garden and truck patch and a nice little orchard which takes Mary and Pless nearly all their time to work it all—which takes three women from the 21 mentioned as able to work— Arthur has to oversee the hands which leaves 15 men to work and 18 women counting the three young girls, and all together 32 hands in the field and several small children that can pick cotton and assist a little, you will know all about them when you look over their ages—Sampson you know is worth very little.

This strange document was not just a listing of property being transferred from one slaveholder to another. It was that and yet something quite different. It was the act of a gentle woman who firmly believed that kind Providence had entrusted "these poor creatures" to her keeping and who was now attempting to pass that trust to others. It was a sincere expression of love, of gratitude, and of motherly anxiety. Yet, after all, each slave was just a piece of property, which in her inventory went along with her acres, her barnyard stock, and her household furniture. This, however, was not her fault, but was the fault of the society in which she lived. Rachel's careful listing of her Negroes and her evident affection for them should not hide the fact that she was, after all, a part of the Cotton Kingdom with its plantations, its labor system, and its way of life. She was also a citizen of the United States with its Declaration of Independence and its Constitution. In an economic sense, she was a capitalist engaged in the effort to make a profit. Success was measured in those terms.

Unfortunately, just now her labor system was under sharp attack, and a line was being drawn between the Northern urban-industrial way of life and that of her agriculturally dominated South. Far to the north, earnest men and women were getting ready to shed their tears and blood to rid the nation of its Rachels. They had never heard of her. They knew only of the society in which she lived. Some were even saying that slavery was a sin. Now and then in Rachel's deep subconscious there might have been a slight evidence of guilt as a slaveholder. It never, however, came to the surface, and she could say sincerely that her Negroes were "born mine and raised chiefly in House with me while small." They were a trust that God had thrust upon her, and it was her duty to make the most of it for all. Slavery was, she thought, less harmful than a wage system that, with indifference, took all and left the worker to find his way both to health and a good life.

Unfortunately God had also "thrust a trust" on John Brown. That complicated matters.

Rachel's next step toward leaving "her house" in order was made when she appeared with Mrs. Moore before James Weems, parish judge and ex officio notary public, to declare and acknowledge that by acts passed before "the Hon. John B. Dawson, Parish Judge on the 16th of March, 1830, and before Robert Widerstrandt, Notary of said Parish of West Feliciana on the 23d of March 1830," she had "bargained, sold, and delivered to her brother David Weeks" all the property and effects "within the plantation on which she resides in the Parish of West Faliciana, together with the slaves and other property and effects for the price of $14,175, which price were well and truly paid to her."

She further declared that it was her intention and the intention of the parties at the time to make good and valid an act of sale. She further declared that she did by her presence fully satisfy and confirm said acts of sale in every respect as if the same had been then legally done and executed. The only reservation was that she should remain on the plantation as long as she lived and take from it "a respectable and comfortable subsistence." She should manage the plantation and other property that she might desire to keep together on the plantation. The interests of David's heirs would thus be protected after her death.

Ill as Rachel was, she kept on with her plans and efforts to keep the plantation in order, the Negroes well cared for, and the crops planted and harvested. Fortunately she had good friends to help as her own strength dwindled. Dr. Denny was with her much of the time, addressing most of her letters and sometimes writing them for her. Her good neighbor William Hargadine found an overseer for her and, when that one proved unsatisfactory, he secured another. He helped Arthur "to gather in the crops" and "attended to the management himself." Rachel commented, "No person ever had a better neighbor. Were he my own son, he could not be more kind, as were also his family." Even when his own wife and children were sickly, he never neglected Rachel. He saw that her needs were met each day.

Not only had Rachel now become totally deaf, but her memory had become bad. There were times when she was certain that she had done something, but when she was able "to reflect a moment" she realized that she had not done it. She could only hope that her friends would understand and that "we shall all meet when the great day comes" and all shall know that "my heart, at least, was true." So, when she was able "to reflect a moment," she brought her will up to date, leaving to David's widow, now Mrs. John Moore, seven undivided twelfths of all her property and to each of his five children one undivided twelfth. Strangely, neither Charlotte nor Clarissa was included, even though they were listed as heirs when the inventory of Rachel's estate was probated.

As the year 1845 came to a close it was apparent that

Rachel had grown weaker and her mind more clouded. With her house in order, her obligations met, and the plantation affairs now in other hands, Rachel for the first time was free to go her own way. She could step aside and look back across the years with pride and satisfaction. Her plantation had grown to a thousand acres and her slaves, not including "that parcel of fine looking children," had reached the seventy-five mark. Her estate was valued at somewhat more than $33,000 (see Appendix II). Few men had done as well. Yet Rachel's pride and satisfaction came more from what she had done for others, black and white, than from what she had been able to do for herself.

Now totally deaf and robbed of all responsibility, Rachel was restless and half sick. Always active and independent she could not now, in spite of handicaps, remain idle and indifferent. Fortunately, Dr. Denny remained with her at all times. It was he who appeared before the Louisiana court on the twentieth day of June, 1846, to "depose and say" that "Mrs. Rachel O'Connor, late of the Parish of the State aforesaid, departed this life near the town of Memphis, Tennessee, on the twenty-second day of May, 1846, the said witness being with the said Rachel O'Connor at the time of her death." This brief, unemotional legal document tells all that is known of Rachel's last days.

For the historian that is not enough. Here was a Southern woman whose life-span covered most of what we call the pre–Civil War era, a woman who had created a self-sufficient economic institution with Negro artisans—carpenters and masons—and Negro overseers, who had planted and harvested the crops more efficiently than any white man had ever done.

With the economic establishment went a social order, in which respect and affection dominated and racial differences were largely ignored. In fact, here in the South Rachel and her kind had, perhaps unconsciously, launched an attack on the institution of Negro slavery. They had developed large plantations where the Negroes were largely born and reared and had taught the skills that forced a degree of equality and interdependence, whether recognized or not. Rachel had paid Arthur a salary when he took over the job of overseer on her plantation, and she had paid cash for the excess produce that her women had raised in their gardens. She made certain that those who had served her faithfully should, after her death, be given their freedom. In other words, slavery had disintegrated at a rapid rate in Rachel's hands. How widely her example had spread throughout the South we do not know. What the use of machinery and the hiring out of slaves to industry might have added is only a guess. All we know as a certainty is that a bloody Civil War and a messy Reconstruction were the methods used to rid a nation of a great social-economic evil. Was that the only way?

In Retrospect

Unique as was Rachel O'Connor's life, she was still a Southern woman in every sense of the words. Circumstances only brought out and exaggerated innate qualities that characterized most of the women who dwelt under the unique Southern physical, social, and economic environment in antebellum days.

Southern women lived closer to and understood better the Southern Negro than did most of their menfolk. White women and black women dealt with each other as individuals in the home, not as gangs under an overseer in the fields. They were together in the quarters when Negro children were born and had a direct hand in raising them until they were able to assume some station in the larger social-economic order. White women looked after the sick—men, women and children—when "the doctor" was not on hand, and "Little Miss" was often the closest tie between the two races in the days that followed.

Like Rachel, when their men left them all alone in Civil War days, Southern women took over and went ahead. There was no economic collapse, no sudden slave uprising or breakdown of the social order. Planting and harvesting, altered to fit needs, continued, and women took over the tasks that once belonged only to men. There was too much of Rachel in Southern womanhood to accept a cause as lost until it was in fact lost. Even then the Southern woman was the last to yield things Southern. Only when the industrial revolution invaded the South and "progress" became the cry did *she* begrudgingly yield old values.

Why did I not write a formal biography of Rachel? I had at first intended to do so but, after a rather long and extensive search, I found that there was only one available source to be used, the letters she had once written to her half brother David Weeks. I had found and copied these long ago. My first reaction was to drop the matter, but I had become so much interested in Rachel that I owed her something. This little book is the result.

The other question is, Why was Rachel up near Memphis at the time of death? She was always apprehensive of steamboat accidents. So why should one who trembled when her friends went "aboard any of the steam boats" now take the long journey upriver to Memphis? Why should one who had so positively stated her determination to die in her own home now take the almost certain chance of dying away from home? One can only guess. Some have suggested that she was searching for another one of those Swayze parcels of land that she, on other occasions, had sought and found. Some have thought that it might have been a matter of health or an effort to escape the heat. The more daring have surmised that this was the first stage in a longer voyage that would have brought her to rest beside her beloved brother David, long asleep in foreign soil. If so, he met her along the way.

Appendix I

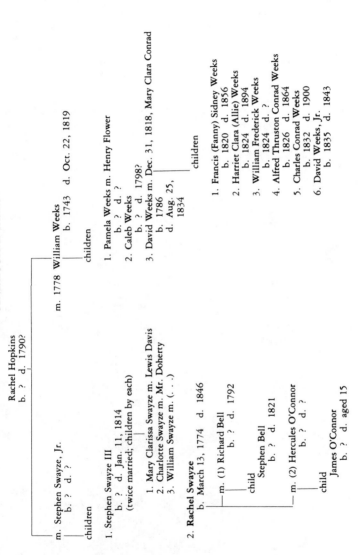

GENEALOGICAL CHART

Rachel Hopkins
b. ? d. 1790?

m. 1778 William Weeks
b. 1743   d. Oct. 22, 1819

children

1. Stephen Swayze, Jr.
b. ? d. ?

children

1. Stephen Swayze III
b. ? d. Jan. 11, 1814
(twice married; children by each)

1. Mary Clarissa Swayze m. Lewis Davis
2. Charlotte Swayze m. Mr. Doherty
3. William Swayze m. (. .)

2. **Rachel Swayze**
b. March 13, 1774   d. 1846

m. (1) Richard Bell
b. ? d. 1792

child
Stephen Bell
b. ? d. 1821

m. (2) Hercules O'Connor
b. ? d. ?

child
James O'Connor
b. ? d. aged 15

1. Pamela Weeks m. Henry Flower
b. ? d. ?
2. Caleb Weeks
b. ? d. 1798?
3. David Weeks m. Dec. 31, 1818, Mary Clara Conrad
b. 1786
d. Aug. 25,
1834

children

1. Francis (Fanny) Sidney Weeks
b. 1820   d. 1856
2. Harriet Clara (Allie) Weeks
b. 1824   d. 1894
3. William Frederick Weeks
b. 1824   d. ?
4. Alfred Thruston Conrad Weeks
b. 1826   d. 1864
5. Charles Conrad Weeks
b. 1832   d. 1900
6. David Weeks, Jr.
b. 1835   d. 1843

Appendix II

Copy of Inventory in the Succession of Mrs. Rachael O'Connor, Deceased.

State of Louisiana,
Parish of West Feliciana.

Be it remembered, that on this 4th. day of June, A.D. 1846, I, James I. Weems, Parish Judge of said Parish, and ex-officio Notary Public, in and for the same have pursuant to an order of the Court of Probates of said Parish, attended at the late residence of Mrs. Rachael O'Connor, late of said Parish and State, deceased, for the purpose of making an inventory of all the property belonging to her Succession. The heirs of said deceased, namely: William L. Swayze, Charlotte Doherty, wife of Anthony Doherty, Julia Ann Scott, Mary C. Davis, Sydney Flower, and William Flower, Jr., residing in this Parish, were duly notified of the time & place of taking this Inventory and are now present, and I have appointed James R. Dupree and William Hargadine, freeholders of said Parish, over the age of twenty one years, as experts and appraisers, who are now present and have taken & subscribed the oath required by law, to-wit:

State of Louisiana,
Parish of West Feliciana.

We, James R. Dupree and William Hargadine, the above named experts and appraisers, having been first duly sworn, according to law, do make oath that we will justly and impartially discharge and perform all and singular the duties incumbent on us as Experts and appraisers of the property belonging to the Succession of Rachael O'Connor, deceased, to the best of our knowledge and understanding, so help us God.

(Signed) James R. Dupree.
(Signed) William Hargadine.

Sworn to and subscribed before
me this 4th. day of June, A.D.
1846.

Jas. I. Weems, Parish Judge.

And John C. Boone and Philander A. Smith, both residents of said Parish of West Feliciana, over the age of twenty-one years, have attended and acted, as witnesses at the making of this Inventory, and sign hereto as such.

The following is a true proces verbal of this Inventory, to-wit:

One tract of land situate in said Parish of West Feliciana, being
the late residence of the deceased, and containing about One
Thousand acres of land, was appraised to be worth the sum of
Three Dollars per acre, making for the whole the sum of
Three Thousand Dollars, $ 3,000.00

Woman named Harriet aged about 45 years, was appraised at
   three hundred and fifty dollars,   350.00
Man named Peter, child of Harriet, aged about 23
   years, was appraised at Six Hundred & fifty dollars,   650.00
Man named Lewis, child of Harriet, aged 20 years, was appraised at Six hundred & fifty dollars,   650.00

Amount carried forward,	$ 4,650.00
Amount brought forward,	$ 4,650.00

Woman named Rose, child of Harriet, aged 15
   years, was appraised at Five Hundred
   dollars,   500.00
Girl named Little Minter, child of
   Harriet, age 13 years was appraised at
   Four hundred and fifty dollars,   450.00
Girl named Mary Ann, child of Harriet,
   aged 10 years, was appraised at Two hundred
   & fifty dollars,   250.00
Boy named Rixum, child of Harriet, aged 7 years,
   was appraised at two hundred dollars,   200.00
Girl named Little Harriet, child of
   Harriet, aged 5 years was appraised at one
   hundred & fifty dollars,   150.00
Man named Eben, aged 30 years, was appraised
   at five hundred & fifty dollars,   550.00
Woman, named Fanny, aged 23 years, was
   appraised at five hundred dollars,   500.00
Boy named Ben, child of Fanny, aged 6 years,
   was appraised at two hundred dollars,   200.00
Boy named Luther, child of Fanny, aged 4 years,
   was appraised at one hundred & fifty dollars,   150.00
Man named Arthur, aged 47 years, was

appraised at four hundred & fifty dollars,	450.00
Woman named Little Milly, aged 41 years, was	
appraised at four hundred dollars,	400.00
Man named Mush, aged 50 years, was appraised	
at three hundred dollars,	300.00

Amount carried forward,	$ 8,750.00
Amount brought forward,	$ 8,750.00
Woman named Pleasant, aged 47 years, was	
appraised at three hundred dollars,	300.00
Man, Bob, aged 47 years, appraised at six	
hundred & fifty dollars	650.00
Man, Littleton, aged 36 years, appraised	
at six hundred and fifty dollars,	650.00
Woman, Caroline, aged 35 years, appraised at	
four hundred dollars,	400.00
Woman, Rhoda, aged 18 years, appraised at five	
hundred dollars,	500.00
Woman, Milly, aged 70 years, appraised at	
fifty dollars,	50.00
Man, Eli, aged 55 years, appraised at seventy	
five dollars,	75.00
Man, Frank, aged 32 years, appraised at six	
hundred & fifty dollars,	650.00
Man, Sangy, aged 26 years, appraised at six	
hundred & fifty dollars,	650.00
Woman, Kitty, aged 20 years, appraised at five	
hundred dollars,	500.00
Girl, Little Ann, child of Kitty, aged 2	
years, appraised at one hundred dollars,	100.00
Man, Dave, aged 36 years, appraised at five	
hundred & fifty dollars,	550.00
Woman, Big Ann, aged 23 years, appraised at	
Four hundred & fifty dollars,	450.00

Amount carried forward,	$14,275.00
Amount brought forward,	$14,275.00
Little Katherine, child of Big Ann, aged	
9 years, appraised at two hundred dollars,	200.00
Woman, Patience, aged 65 years, appraised at	
one hundred dollars,	100.00
Man, John, aged 40 years, appraised at five	
hundred & fifty dollars,	550.00

Man, Sampson, aged 40 years, appraised at
three hundred & fifty dollars, 350.00
Woman, Bridget, aged 35 years, appraised at
five hundred dollars, 500.00
Woman, Celeste, child of Bridget, aged 16
years, appraised at three hundred
dollars, 300.00
Girl, Little Patience, child of Bridget,
aged 9 years, appraised at three
hundred dollars, 300.00
Girl, Celia, child of Bridget, aged 7 years,
appraised at two hundred & twenty-five
dollars, 225.00
Girl, Susan, child of Bridget, aged 2 years,
appraised at One hundred dollars, 100.00
Woman, Maria, aged 27 years, appraised at
five hundred dollars, 500.00
Girl, Silvia, child of Maria, aged 12 years,
was appraised at three hundred dollars, 300.00
Girl, Louise, child of Maria, aged 8 years,
appraised at two hundred & fifty dollars, 250.00
Girl, Delphine, child of Maria, aged 6
years, appraised at one hundred & seventy
five dollars, 175.00
Girl, Nellie, child of Maria, aged 4 years,
appraised at one [hundred] & fifty dollars, 150.00

Amount carried forward, $18,275.00
Amount brought forward, $18,275.00

Girl, Little Caroline, child of Maria,
aged 3 years, appraised at one hundred
and twenty-five dollars, 125.00
Girl, Nanny, child of Maria, aged 7 months,
appraised at one hundred dollars, 100.00
Woman, Jenny, aged 34 years, appraised at Five
hundred dollars, 500.00
Little Betsy, child of Jenny, 15 years,
appraised at Five Hundred Dollars, 500.00
Boy, Lewis, child of Jenny, aged 4 years,
appraised at two hundred & twenty five
dollars, 225.00
Girl, Emily, child of Jenny, aged 3 years,
appraised at one hundred & fifty dollars, 150.00

Girl, Little Hettie, child of Jenny, age 1
    year, appraised at one hundred dollars,   100.00
Woman, Leah, aged 19 years, appraised at five
    hundred dollars,   500.00
Girl, Winny, child of Leah, aged 6 years, appraised at
    one hundred & seventy five dollars,   175.00
Girl, Ritta, child of Leah, aged 4 years, appraised at one
    hundred & fifty dollars,   150.00
Boy, Daniel, child of Leah, aged 2 years, appraised at one
    hundred dollars,   100.00
Woman, Julia, age 26 years, appraised at five hundred
    dollars,   500.00
Boy, Henry, child of Julia, aged 16 years, appraised at
    five hundred dollars,   500.00

Amount carried forward,	$21,900.00
Amount brought forward,	21,900.00

Boy, Little John, child of Julia, aged 12 years, appraised
    at three hundred dollars,   300.00
Boy, Epex, child of Julia, aged 7 years, appraised at two
    hundred & fifty dollars,   250.00
Girl, Biddy, child of Julia, aged 4 years, appraised at one
    hundred & seventy five dollars,   175.00
Boy, Little Joe, child of Julia, aged 3 years, appraised at one
    hundred & twenty five dollars,   125.00
Woman, Charity, aged 36 years, appraised at five hundred
    dollars,   500.00
Girl, Nancy, child of Charity, aged 15 years, appraised at
    five hundred dollars,   500.00
Girl, Margaret, child of Charity, aged 13 years, appraised
    at four hundred dollars,   400.00
Girl, Frances, child of Charity, aged 10 years, appraised at
    three hundred dollars,   300.00
Girl, Little Mary, child of Charity, aged 6 years, appraised
    at two hundred dollars,   200.00
Girl, Lizzie, child of Charity, aged 4 years, appraised at
    one hundred & fifty dollars,   150.00
Woman, Sarah, aged 37 years, appraised at Four Hundred &
    fifty dollars,   450.00
Man, Ephriam, son of Sarah, aged 19 years, appraised at
    six hundred & fifty dollars,   650.00
Boy, Little Arthur, child of Sarah, aged 5 years, appraised at
    One hundred & seventy five dollars,   175.00

Woman, Matilda, aged 27 years, appraised at five hundred
dollars,   500.00
Woman, Eliza, aged 28 years, appraised at five hundred
dollars,   500.00
Girl, Nanny, child of Eliza, aged 13 years, appraised at three
hundred dollars,   300.00

Amount carried forward,	$27,375.00
Amount brought forward,	$27,375.00

Girl, Jane, aged 8 years, appraised at two hundred
dollars,   200.00
Boy, Alfred, aged 4 years, appraised at one hundred & fifty
dollars,   150.00
Woman, Dinah, aged 60 years, appraised at Fifty
Dollars,   50.00
Woman, Margaret, aged 46 years, appraised at three hundred
dollars,   300.00
Woman, Lydia, aged 38 years, appraised at five hundred
dollars,   500.00
Girl, Martha, child of Lydia, aged 8 years, appraised at two
hundred & fifty dollars,   250.00
Man, Big Joe, aged 30 years, appraised at six hundred & fifty
dollars,   650.00
Man, Big Harry, aged 34 years, appraised at six hundred and
fifty dollars,   650.00
Man, Amos, aged 24 years, appraised at six hundred & fifty
dollars,   650.00
Woman, Minta, aged 60 years, appraised at one hundred
dollars,   100.00

           $30,875.00

PERSONALS

1 side board appraised at Forty dollars,	40.00
1 waiter & dumbell appraised at two dollars,	2.00
2 candle shade, appraised at four dollars,	4.00
1 castor, appraised at five dollars,	5.00
1 parlor table, appraised at fifteen dollars,	15.00

Amount carried forward,	$30,941.00
Amount brought forward,	$30,941.00
1 book case & books, appraised at fifty dollars,	50.00
1 mantle glass, appraised at six dollars,	6.00
1 set office irons, appraised at ten dollars,	10.00

Shovel & tools appraised at two dollars,	2.00
1 sofa, appraised at ten dollars,	10.00
1 secretary appraised at twenty dollars,	20.00
½ doz. cane bottom chairs appraised at four dollars,	4.00
3 curtains, appraised at three dollars,	3.00
1 carpet, appraised at ten dollars,	10.00
1 map appraised at two dollars,	2.00
1 bed stead, bed & furniture, appraised at sixty dollars,	60.00
1 Armoire, appraised at forty dollars,	40.00
1 old desk appraised at three dollars,	3.00
1 mantle glass, appraised at six dollars,	6.00
1 old chair appraised at three dollars,	3.00
1 small pair fire irons, appraised at one dollar,	1.00
1 trundle bed stead, appraised at one dollar,	1.00
1 bed stead, bed & bedding, appraised at thirty dollars,	30.00
1 bed stead, bed & bedding, appraised at twenty five dollars,	25.00
1 bureau, appraised at fifteen dollars,	15.00
1 old bureau, appraised at three dollars,	3.00
2 trunks with books, appraised at ten dollars,	10.00
1 toilet glass, appraised at one dollar,	1.00
1 common carpet, appraised at three dollars,	3.00
1 bed, bed stead & bedding, appraised at thirty dollars,	30.00
Amount carried forward,	$31,289.00
Amount brought forward,	$31,289.00
1 old trundle bed stead & bedding, appraised at eight dollars,	8.00
1 wash stand appraised at one dollar,	1.00
1 old clock, appraised at five dollars,	5.00
1 old side board, appraised at ten dollars,	10.00
1 wire safe, appraised at five dollars,	5.00
1 settee appraised at five dollars,	5.00
2 dining tables, appraised at ten dollars,	10.00
1 Lot of crockery ware, appraised at forty dollars,	40.00
1 lot of knives & forks, appraised at eight dollars,	8.00
Lamps & candle sticks, appraised at two dollars,	2.00
1 armoire, appraised at five dollars,	5.00
1 bed & bed stead, appraised at six dollars,	6.00
8 head of mules, appraised at four hundred and eighty dollars,	480.00
9 head of horses, appraised at three hundred and sixty dollars,	360.00
125 head of cattle, appraised at six hundred dollars,	600.00
65 sheep, appraised at eighty five dollars,	85.00
20 head of hogs, appraised at twenty dollars,	20.00
1 wagon, appraised at twenty dollars,	20.00
1 boat appraised at ten dollars,	10.00

1 market cart, appraised at eight dollars,	8.00

Amount carried forward,	$32,977.00
Amount brought forward,	$32,977.00
1 dozen table spoons, appraised at thirty five dollars,	35.00
1 dozen tea spoons, appraised at seventeen dollars,	17.00
Total Inventory,	$33,029.00

RECAPITULATION

Lands appraised at three thousand dollars,	$ 3,000.00
Negro slaves appraised at twenty seven thousand eight hundred and seventy five dollars,	$27,875.00
Personal property, appraised at two thousand one hundred and fifty four dollars,	$ 2,154.00
Total Inventory,	$33,029.00

And there being no other property shown to be inventoried, therefore I, said Judge & Ex-Officio Notary Public, do now close this inventory amounting to the foregoing sum of thirty-three thousand and twenty nine dollars, and said parties and experts sign hereto in presence of and with John C. Boone and Philander A. Smith, the above named witnesses, and me said Judge and ex-officio Notary Public.

In testimony of all which I grant these presents under my signature and seal official this said 4th. day of June, A.D. 1846.

Witnesses:

J. C. Boone.
P. A. Smith.

(Signed) James R. Dupree.
William Hargadine.
W. L. Swayze.
Charlotte Doherty.
A. Doherty.
Julia Ann Scott.
Mary C. Davis.
Sydney Flower.

Jas. I. Weems,
Parish Judge.

Endorsed: Recorded June 12, 1846, in Book of Inventories "F" pages 134, 140.

I hereby certify that the above and foregoing is a true copy of the original Inventory filed in the Succession of Mrs. Rachael O'Connor, Deceased.

(Signed) Florence F. Holsan

Clerk and Recorder,
Parish of West Feliciana, La.